Digital Forensics
Complete Self-Assessment Guide

CW00521510

The guidance in this Self-Assessment is base
practices and standards in business process ....ure, design and
quality management. The guidance is also based on the professional
judgment of the individual collaborators listed in the Acknowledgments.

Notice of rights

Trademarks

Copyright © by The Art of Service
http://theartofservice.com
service@theartofservice.com

Table of Contents

About The Art of Service

The Art of Service, Business Process Architects since 2000, is dedicated to helping stakeholders achieve excellence.

Defining, designing, creating, and implementing a process to solve a stakeholders challenge or meet an objective is the most valuable role… In EVERY group, company, organization and department.

Unless you're talking a one-time, single-use project, there should be a process. Whether that process is managed and implemented by humans, AI, or a combination of the two, it needs to be designed by someone with a complex enough perspective to ask the right questions.

Someone capable of asking the right questions and step back and say, 'What are we really trying to accomplish here? And is there a different way to look at it?'

With The Art of Service's Standard Requirements Self-Assessments, we empower people who can do just that — whether their title is marketer, entrepreneur, manager, salesperson, consultant, Business Process Manager, executive assistant, IT Manager, CIO etc... —they are the people who rule the future. They are people who watch the process as it happens, and ask the right questions to make the process work better.

Contact us when you need any support with this Self-Assessment and any help with templates, blue-prints and examples of standard documents you might need:

http://theartofservice.com
service@theartofservice.com

Acknowledgments

This checklist was developed under the auspices of The Art of Service, chaired by Gerardus Blokdyk.

Representatives from several client companies participated in the preparation of this Self-Assessment.

In addition, we are thankful for the design and printing services provided.

Included Resources - how to access

Included with your purchase of the book is the Digital Forensics Self-Assessment Spreadsheet Dashboard which contains all questions and Self-Assessment areas and auto-generates insights, graphs, and project RACI planning - all with examples to get you started right away.

How? Simply send an email to
access@theartofservice.com
with this books' title in the subject to get the Digital Forensics Self Assessment Tool right away.

You will receive the following contents with New and Updated specific criteria:

- The latest quick edition of the book in PDF

- The latest complete edition of the book in PDF, which criteria correspond to the criteria in...

- The Self-Assessment Excel Dashboard, and...

- Example pre-filled Self-Assessment Excel Dashboard to get familiar with results generation

- In-depth specific Checklists covering the topic

- Project management checklists and templates to assist with implementation

INCLUDES LIFETIME SELF ASSESSMENT UPDATES

Every self assessment comes with Lifetime Updates and Lifetime Free Updated Books. Lifetime Updates is an industry-first feature which allows you to receive verified self assessment updates, ensuring you always have the most accurate information at your fingertips.

Get it now- you will be glad you did - do it now, before you forget.

Send an email to **access@theartofservice.com** with this books' title in the subject to get the Digital Forensics Self Assessment Tool right away.

Your feedback is invaluable to us

If you recently bought this book, we would love to hear from you! You can do this by writing a review on amazon (or the online store where you purchased this book) about your last purchase! As part of our continual service improvement process, we love to hear real client experiences and feedback.

How does it work?
To post a review on Amazon, just log in to your account and click on the Create Your Own Review button (under Customer Reviews) of the relevant product page. You can find examples of product reviews in Amazon. If you purchased from another online store, simply follow their procedures.

What happens when I submit my review?
Once you have submitted your review, send us an email at review@theartofservice.com with the link to your review so we can properly thank you for your feedback.

Purpose of this Self-Assessment

This Self-Assessment has been developed to improve understanding of the requirements and elements of Digital Forensics, based on best practices and standards in business process architecture, design and quality management.

It is designed to allow for a rapid Self-Assessment to determine how closely existing management practices and procedures correspond to the elements of the Self-Assessment.

The criteria of requirements and elements of Digital Forensics have been rephrased in the format of a Self-Assessment questionnaire, with a seven-criterion scoring system, as explained in this document.

In this format, even with limited background knowledge of Digital

Forensics, a manager can quickly review existing operations to determine how they measure up to the standards. This in turn can serve as the starting point of a 'gap analysis' to identify management tools or system elements that might usefully be implemented in the organization to help improve overall performance.

How to use the Self-Assessment

On the following pages are a series of questions to identify to what extent your Digital Forensics initiative is complete in comparison to the requirements set in standards.

To facilitate answering the questions, there is a space in front of each question to enter a score on a scale of '1' to '5'.

1 Strongly Disagree

2 Disagree

3 Neutral

4 Agree

5 Strongly Agree

Read the question and rate it with the following in front of mind:

'In my belief,
the answer to this question is clearly defined'.

There are two ways in which you can choose to interpret this statement;
1. how aware are you that the answer to the question is clearly defined
2. for more in-depth analysis you can choose to gather

evidence and confirm the answer to the question. This obviously will take more time, most Self-Assessment users opt for the first way to interpret the question and dig deeper later on based on the outcome of the overall Self-Assessment.

A score of '1' would mean that the answer is not clear at all, where a '5' would mean the answer is crystal clear and defined. Leave emtpy when the question is not applicable or you don't want to answer it, you can skip it without affecting your score. Write your score in the space provided.

After you have responded to all the appropriate statements in each section, compute your average score for that section, using the formula provided, and round to the nearest tenth. Then transfer to the corresponding spoke in the Digital Forensics Scorecard on the second next page of the Self-Assessment.

Your completed Digital Forensics Scorecard will give you a clear presentation of which Digital Forensics areas need attention.

Digital Forensics Scorecard Example

Example of how the finalized Scorecard can look like:

Digital Forensics Scorecard

Your Scores:

BEGINNING OF THE SELF-ASSESSMENT:

CRITERION #1: RECOGNIZE

INTENT: Be aware of the need for change. Recognize that there is an unfavorable variation, problem or symptom.

In my belief, the answer to this question is clearly defined:

5 Strongly Agree

4 Agree

3 Neutral

2 Disagree

1 Strongly Disagree

1. Consider your own Digital Forensics project, what types of organizational problems do you think might be causing or affecting your problem, based on the work done so far?
<--- Score

2. What tools and technologies are needed for a custom Digital Forensics project?
<--- Score

3. Are there any revenue recognition issues?
<--- Score

4. What are your needs in relation to Digital Forensics skills, labor, equipment, and markets?
<--- Score

5. Are there Digital Forensics problems defined?
<--- Score

6. What is the smallest subset of the problem you can usefully solve?
<--- Score

7. Can management personnel recognize the monetary benefit of Digital Forensics?
<--- Score

8. As a sponsor, customer or management, how important is it to meet goals, objectives?
<--- Score

9. What are the issues of law and issues of fact?
<--- Score

10. Will a response program recognize when a crisis occurs and provide some level of response?
<--- Score

11. What would happen if Digital Forensics weren't done?
<--- Score

12. To what extent does each concerned units management team recognize Digital Forensics as an

effective investment?
<--- Score

13. What else needs to be measured?
<--- Score

14. What problems are you facing and how do you consider Digital Forensics will circumvent those obstacles?
<--- Score

15. Do you have/need 24-hour access to key personnel?
<--- Score

16. What extra resources will you need?
<--- Score

17. Does Digital Forensics create potential expectations in other areas that need to be recognized and considered?
<--- Score

18. How do you take a forward-looking perspective in identifying Digital Forensics research related to market response and models?
<--- Score

19. How much are sponsors, customers, partners, stakeholders involved in Digital Forensics? In other words, what are the risks, if Digital Forensics does not deliver successfully?
<--- Score

20. What is the problem or issue?
<--- Score

21. How does it fit into your organizational needs and tasks?
<--- Score

22. Are there recognized Digital Forensics problems?
<--- Score

23. Is it clear when you think of the day ahead of you what activities and tasks you need to complete?
<--- Score

24. Who needs to know about Digital Forensics?
<--- Score

25. Who needs what information?
<--- Score

26. Can you see any problems with the investigation?
<--- Score

27. What information do users need?
<--- Score

28. How are you going to measure success?
<--- Score

29. Looking at each person individually – does every one have the qualities which are needed to work in this group?
<--- Score

30. Does your organization need more Digital Forensics education?
<--- Score

31. Timeline of an entire event for presentation (When) - can the entire story board re-constructed?

<--- Score

32. What are the timeframes required to resolve each of the issues/problems?

<--- Score

33. For your Digital Forensics project, identify and describe the business environment, is there more than one layer to the business environment?

<--- Score

34. What situation(s) led to this Digital Forensics Self Assessment?

<--- Score

35. Are employees recognized or rewarded for performance that demonstrates the highest levels of integrity?

<--- Score

36. Who had the original idea?

<--- Score

37. How can auditing be a preventative security measure?

<--- Score

38. What vendors make products that address the Digital Forensics needs?

<--- Score

39. Are controls defined to recognize and contain

problems?

<--- Score

40. Are you dealing with any of the same issues today as yesterday? What can you do about this?

<--- Score

41. Do you need to avoid or amend any Digital Forensics activities?

<--- Score

42. How do you identify the kinds of information that you will need?

<--- Score

43. What do you need to start doing?

<--- Score

44. Are problem definition and motivation clearly presented?

<--- Score

45. What needs to be done?

<--- Score

46. What are the expected benefits of Digital Forensics to the business?

<--- Score

47. Who are your key stakeholders who need to sign off?

<--- Score

48. What are the minority interests and what amount of minority interests can be recognized?

<--- Score

49. Should you invest in industry-recognized qualications?
<--- Score

50. What are the business objectives to be achieved with Digital Forensics?
<--- Score

51. Are there any specific expectations or concerns about the Digital Forensics team, Digital Forensics itself?
<--- Score

52. Are your goals realistic? Do you need to redefine your problem? Perhaps the problem has changed or maybe you have reached your goal and need to set a new one?
<--- Score

53. Will new equipment/products be required to facilitate Digital Forensics delivery, for example is new software needed?
<--- Score

54. What does Digital Forensics success mean to the stakeholders?
<--- Score

55. How are the Digital Forensics's objectives aligned to the organization's overall business strategy?
<--- Score

56. Who needs to be involved and to what extent?
<--- Score

57. How do you assess your Digital Forensics workforce capability and capacity needs, including skills, competencies, and staffing levels?
<--- Score

58. What prevents you from making the changes you know will make you a more effective Digital Forensics leader?
<--- Score

59. Who else hopes to benefit from it?
<--- Score

60. Think about the people you identified for your Digital Forensics project and the project responsibilities you would assign to them. what kind of training do you think they would need to perform these responsibilities effectively?
<--- Score

61. What training and capacity building actions are needed to implement proposed reforms?
<--- Score

62. Do you know what you need to know about Digital Forensics?
<--- Score

63. Will Digital Forensics deliverables need to be tested and, if so, by whom?
<--- Score

64. When a Digital Forensics manager recognizes a problem, what options are available?
<--- Score

65. Will it solve real problems?
<--- Score

66. Who defines the rules in relation to any given issue?
<--- Score

67. Do you need different information or graphics?
<--- Score

68. What should be considered when identifying available resources, constraints, and deadlines?
<--- Score

69. To what extent would your organization benefit from being recognized as a award recipient?
<--- Score

Add up total points for this section:
_ _ _ _ _ = Total points for this section

Divided by: _ _ _ _ _ _ (number of statements answered) = _ _ _ _ _ _
Average score for this section

Transfer your score to the Digital Forensics Index at the beginning of the Self-Assessment.

CRITERION #2: DEFINE:

INTENT: Formulate the business problem. Define the problem, needs and objectives.

In my belief, the answer to this question is clearly defined:

5 Strongly Agree

4 Agree

3 Neutral

2 Disagree

1 Strongly Disagree

1. Are resources adequate for the scope?
<--- Score

2. How do you hand over Digital Forensics context?
<--- Score

3. How is the team tracking and documenting its work?
<--- Score

4. Have specific policy objectives been defined?
<--- Score

5. Do the problem and goal statements meet the SMART criteria (specific, measurable, attainable, relevant, and time-bound)?
<--- Score

6. What other organization(s) should be contacted to mitigate potential cases of identity theft?
<--- Score

7. What are the dynamics of the communication plan?
<--- Score

8. What system do you use for gathering Digital Forensics information?
<--- Score

9. What key business process output measure(s) does Digital Forensics leverage and how?
<--- Score

10. How will variation in the actual durations of each activity be dealt with to ensure that the expected Digital Forensics results are met?
<--- Score

11. What is out of scope?
<--- Score

12. How would you define digital forensics and in your opinion how is it different from cyber investigations?
<--- Score

13. Are task requirements clearly defined?
<--- Score

14. Has the direction changed at all during the course of Digital Forensics? If so, when did it change and why?
<--- Score

15. Do you all define Digital Forensics in the same way?
<--- Score

16. Is Digital Forensics required?
<--- Score

17. Are improvement team members fully trained on Digital Forensics?
<--- Score

18. What is out-of-scope initially?
<--- Score

19. When should the case be presented?
<--- Score

20. When was the Digital Forensics start date?
<--- Score

21. How do you think the partners involved in Digital Forensics would have defined success?
<--- Score

22. How and when will the baselines be defined?
<--- Score

23. Has the Digital Forensics work been fairly and/ or equitably divided and delegated among team members who are qualified and capable to perform the work? Has everyone contributed?
<--- Score

24. What are the rough order estimates on cost savings/opportunities that Digital Forensics brings?
<--- Score

25. Is the improvement team aware of the different versions of a process: what they think it is vs. what it actually is vs. what it should be vs. what it could be?
<--- Score

26. What would be the goal or target for a Digital Forensics's improvement team?
<--- Score

27. In what way can you redefine the criteria of choice clients have in your category in your favor?
<--- Score

28. Are business processes mapped?
<--- Score

29. How did the Digital Forensics manager receive input to the development of a Digital Forensics improvement plan and the estimated completion dates/times of each activity?
<--- Score

30. Is it clearly defined in and to your organization what you do?
<--- Score

31. What are the boundaries of the scope? What is in bounds and what is not? What is the start point? What is the stop point?
<--- Score

32. What sources do you use to gather information for a Digital Forensics study?
<--- Score

33. Has a project plan, Gantt chart, or similar been developed/completed?
<--- Score

34. Are roles and responsibilities formally defined?
<--- Score

35. Have all basic functions of Digital Forensics been defined?
<--- Score

36. Who is gathering Digital Forensics information?
<--- Score

37. Is full participation by members in regularly held team meetings guaranteed?
<--- Score

38. Why are you doing Digital Forensics and what is the scope?
<--- Score

39. What oversight is required by management?
<--- Score

40. What are the tasks and definitions?
<--- Score

41. Are there any constraints known that bear on the ability to perform Digital Forensics work? How is the team addressing them?
<--- Score

42. What customer feedback methods were used to solicit their input?
<--- Score

43. Has anyone else (internal or external to the organization) attempted to solve this problem or a similar one before? If so, what knowledge can be leveraged from these previous efforts?
<--- Score

44. Is there a completed SIPOC representation, describing the Suppliers, Inputs, Process, Outputs, and Customers?
<--- Score

45. When is the estimated completion date?
<--- Score

46. Does the team have regular meetings?
<--- Score

47. Has everyone on the team, including the team leaders, been properly trained?
<--- Score

48. What are the Roles and Responsibilities for each team member and its leadership? Where is this documented?
<--- Score

49. How do you gather Digital Forensics requirements?
<--- Score

50. Are required metrics defined, what are they?
<--- Score

51. Has a high-level 'as is' process map been completed, verified and validated?
<--- Score

52. Is a fully trained team formed, supported, and committed to work on the Digital Forensics improvements?
<--- Score

53. How can the value of Digital Forensics be defined?
<--- Score

54. Will team members regularly document their Digital Forensics work?
<--- Score

55. Is the team sponsored by a champion or business leader?
<--- Score

56. Who defines (or who defined) the rules and roles?
<--- Score

57. Have all of the relationships been defined properly?
<--- Score

58. What is the scope of the Digital Forensics effort?
<--- Score

59. What are the record-keeping requirements of Digital Forensics activities?
<--- Score

60. Are audit criteria, scope, frequency and methods defined?
<--- Score

61. Is there a critical path to deliver Digital Forensics results?
<--- Score

62. Scope of sensitive information?
<--- Score

63. Who are the Digital Forensics improvement team members, including Management Leads and Coaches?
<--- Score

64. Are there different segments of customers?
<--- Score

65. Has/have the customer(s) been identified?
<--- Score

66. Is any warrant, search warrant required?
<--- Score

67. What critical content must be communicated – who, what, when, where, and how?
<--- Score

68. If substitutes have been appointed, have they been briefed on the Digital Forensics goals and

received regular communications as to the progress to date?
<--- Score

69. How would you define the culture at your organization, how susceptible is it to Digital Forensics changes?
<--- Score

70. Is the team equipped with available and reliable resources?
<--- Score

71. How often are the team meetings?
<--- Score

72. Has your scope been defined?
<--- Score

73. What constraints exist that might impact the team?
<--- Score

74. What was the context?
<--- Score

75. Is the team formed and are team leaders (Coaches and Management Leads) assigned?
<--- Score

76. What is the context?
<--- Score

77. Is there regularly 100% attendance at the team meetings? If not, have appointed substitutes attended to preserve cross-functionality and full

representation?
<--- Score

78. Will team members perform Digital Forensics work when assigned and in a timely fashion?
<--- Score

79. What is the scope of Digital Forensics?
<--- Score

80. What defines best in class?
<--- Score

81. How will the Digital Forensics team and the organization measure complete success of Digital Forensics?
<--- Score

82. Has the improvement team collected the 'voice of the customer' (obtained feedback – qualitative and quantitative)?
<--- Score

83. What is in the scope and what is not in scope?
<--- Score

84. Are accountability and ownership for Digital Forensics clearly defined?
<--- Score

85. Is Digital Forensics linked to key business goals and objectives?
<--- Score

86. What is the required and related information?
<--- Score

87. What happens if Digital Forensics's scope changes?
<--- Score

88. How was the 'as is' process map developed, reviewed, verified and validated?
<--- Score

89. When are meeting minutes sent out? Who is on the distribution list?
<--- Score

90. What Digital Forensics requirements should be gathered?
<--- Score

91. Are different versions of process maps needed to account for the different types of inputs?
<--- Score

92. Does the scope remain the same?
<--- Score

93. What baselines are required to be defined and managed?
<--- Score

94. Are customers identified and high impact areas defined?
<--- Score

95. Are approval levels defined for contracts and supplements to contracts?
<--- Score

96. Is data collected and displayed to better

understand customer(s) critical needs and requirements.
<--- Score

97. What specifically is the problem? Where does it occur? When does it occur? What is its extent?
<--- Score

98. Is there a completed, verified, and validated high-level 'as is' (not 'should be' or 'could be') business process map?
<--- Score

99. What is the definition of success?
<--- Score

100. What is in scope?
<--- Score

101. Is the Digital Forensics scope complete and appropriately sized?
<--- Score

102. Is there a Digital Forensics management charter, including business case, problem and goal statements, scope, milestones, roles and responsibilities, communication plan?
<--- Score

103. Are team charters developed?
<--- Score

104. Are customer(s) identified and segmented according to their different needs and requirements?
<--- Score

105. What are the compelling business reasons for embarking on Digital Forensics?
<--- Score

106. What scope to assess?
<--- Score

107. Has a team charter been developed and communicated?
<--- Score

108. Is scope creep really all bad news?
<--- Score

109. Is the current 'as is' process being followed? If not, what are the discrepancies?
<--- Score

110. How do you manage scope?
<--- Score

111. Is Digital Forensics currently on schedule according to the plan?
<--- Score

112. How do you keep key subject matter experts in the loop?
<--- Score

113. How does the Digital Forensics manager ensure against scope creep?
<--- Score

114. Have the customer needs been translated into specific, measurable requirements? How?
<--- Score

115. Is the Digital Forensics scope manageable?
<--- Score

116. Is the scope of Digital Forensics defined?
<--- Score

117. Is the team adequately staffed with the desired cross-functionality? If not, what additional resources are available to the team?
<--- Score

Add up total points for this section:
_ _ _ _ _ = Total points for this section

Divided by: _ _ _ _ _ _ (number of statements answered) = _ _ _ _ _ _
Average score for this section

Transfer your score to the Digital Forensics Index at the beginning of the Self-Assessment.

CRITERION #3: MEASURE:

INTENT: Gather the correct data.
Measure the current performance and
evolution of the situation.

In my belief, the answer to this
question is clearly defined:

5 Strongly Agree

4 Agree

3 Neutral

2 Disagree

1 Strongly Disagree

1. Is long term and short term variability accounted for?
<--- Score

2. How to cause the change?
<--- Score

3. What are the key input variables? What are the key process variables? What are the key output variables?

<--- Score

4. Is Process Variation Displayed/Communicated?
<--- Score

5. Did you tackle the cause or the symptom?
<--- Score

6. How will your organization measure success?
<--- Score

7. What potential environmental factors impact the Digital Forensics effort?
<--- Score

8. What is an unallowable cost?
<--- Score

9. How is progress measured?
<--- Score

10. What are your key Digital Forensics indicators that you will measure, analyze and track?
<--- Score

11. What measurements are being captured?
<--- Score

12. How can you measure the performance?
<--- Score

13. Why do the measurements/indicators matter?
<--- Score

14. Is data collection planned and executed?
<--- Score

15. What relevant entities could be measured?
<--- Score

16. Does Digital Forensics analysis isolate the fundamental causes of problems?
<--- Score

17. What changes could be made to the organizationís policies, guidelines, and procedures to reduce the impact of similar future incidents?
<--- Score

18. Have the types of risks that may impact Digital Forensics been identified and analyzed?
<--- Score

19. Are key measures identified and agreed upon?
<--- Score

20. Are there any easy-to-implement alternatives to Digital Forensics? Sometimes other solutions are available that do not require the cost implications of a full-blown project?
<--- Score

21. What causes extra work or rework?
<--- Score

22. What is the right balance of time and resources between investigation, analysis, and discussion and dissemination?
<--- Score

23. Is a solid data collection plan established that includes measurement systems analysis?

<--- Score

24. Which measures and indicators matter?
<--- Score

25. How will you measure your Digital Forensics effectiveness?
<--- Score

26. What could cause delays in the schedule?
<--- Score

27. Does the Digital Forensics task fit the client's priorities?
<--- Score

28. How do your measurements capture actionable Digital Forensics information for use in exceeding your customers expectations and securing your customers engagement?
<--- Score

29. How will measures be used to manage and adapt?
<--- Score

30. How large is the gap between current performance and the customer-specified (goal) performance?
<--- Score

31. What charts has the team used to display the components of variation in the process?
<--- Score

32. What evidence is there and what is measured?
<--- Score

33. Are process variation components displayed/
communicated using suitable charts, graphs, plots?
<--- Score

34. Can you do Digital Forensics without complex
(expensive) analysis?
<--- Score

35. What are the costs of reform?
<--- Score

**36. Credible and/or Competent: Is the information
believable, trustworthy, and true and, if so, by
what measure?**
<--- Score

37. What causes innovation to fail or succeed in your
organization?
<--- Score

38. How do you aggregate measures across priorities?
<--- Score

39. How frequently do you track Digital Forensics
measures?
<--- Score

40. What has the team done to assure the stability and
accuracy of the measurement process?
<--- Score

41. Have the concerns of stakeholders to help identify
and define potential barriers been obtained and
analyzed?
<--- Score

42. Are missed Digital Forensics opportunities costing your organization money?
<--- Score

43. How is performance measured?
<--- Score

44. What would be a real cause for concern?
<--- Score

45. The approach of traditional Digital Forensics works for detail complexity but is focused on a systematic approach rather than an understanding of the nature of systems themselves, what approach will permit your organization to deal with the kind of unpredictable emergent behaviors that dynamic complexity can introduce?
<--- Score

46. What disadvantage does this cause for the user?
<--- Score

47. How do you control the overall costs of your work processes?
<--- Score

48. Among the Digital Forensics product and service cost to be estimated, which is considered hardest to estimate?
<--- Score

49. What legal considerations should the analysts be aware of if they want to examine a data source that the organization does not own?
<--- Score

50. Does Digital Forensics analysis show the relationships among important Digital Forensics factors?
<--- Score

51. Are high impact defects defined and identified in the business process?
<--- Score

52. Why do you expend time and effort to implement measurement, for whom?
<--- Score

53. What harm might be caused?
<--- Score

54. What are your customers expectations and measures?
<--- Score

55. Are there measurements based on task performance?
<--- Score

56. What is measured? Why?
<--- Score

57. What particular quality tools did the team find helpful in establishing measurements?
<--- Score

58. How are measurements made?
<--- Score

59. Do staff have the necessary skills to collect,

analyze, and report data?
<--- Score

60. How will effects be measured?
<--- Score

61. Are the measurements objective?
<--- Score

62. What key measures identified indicate the performance of the business process?
<--- Score

63. How do you measure variability?
<--- Score

64. What data was collected (past, present, future/ ongoing)?
<--- Score

65. How do you measure success?
<--- Score

66. How do you measure efficient delivery of Digital Forensics services?
<--- Score

67. Is key measure data collection planned and executed, process variation displayed and communicated and performance baselined?
<--- Score

68. Are you aware of what could cause a problem?
<--- Score

69. What are the uncertainties surrounding estimates

of impact?

<--- Score

70. Can you measure the return on analysis?

<--- Score

71. What are your key Digital Forensics organizational performance measures, including key short and longer-term financial measures?

<--- Score

72. How is the value delivered by Digital Forensics being measured?

<--- Score

73. How do you measure lifecycle phases?

<--- Score

74. What causes mismanagement?

<--- Score

75. What do you measure and why?

<--- Score

76. Are the units of measure consistent?

<--- Score

77. What are the agreed upon definitions of the high impact areas, defect(s), unit(s), and opportunities that will figure into the process capability metrics?

<--- Score

78. How do you stay flexible and focused to recognize larger Digital Forensics results?

<--- Score

79. How do you identify and analyze stakeholders and their interests?
<--- Score

80. Where does the emerging discipline of computer forensics, or the even less understood area of network forensics, fit into the needs of computer analysis?
<--- Score

81. How will you measure success?
<--- Score

82. Have you made assumptions about the shape of the future, particularly its impact on your customers and competitors?
<--- Score

83. Are you taking your company in the direction of better and revenue or cheaper and cost?
<--- Score

84. Are losses documented, analyzed, and remedial processes developed to prevent future losses?
<--- Score

85. Do you effectively measure and reward individual and team performance?
<--- Score

86. What methods are feasible and acceptable to estimate the impact of reforms?
<--- Score

87. Is there a Performance Baseline?
<--- Score

88. Which stakeholder characteristics are analyzed?
<--- Score

89. How can you measure Digital Forensics in a systematic way?
<--- Score

90. Have changes been properly/adequately analyzed for effect?
<--- Score

91. How do you do risk analysis of rare, cascading, catastrophic events?
<--- Score

92. Is data collected on key measures that were identified?
<--- Score

93. What could cause you to change course?
<--- Score

94. How will success or failure be measured?
<--- Score

95. Does your organization systematically track and analyze outcomes related for accountability and quality improvement?
<--- Score

96. Who should receive measurement reports?
<--- Score

97. Does Digital Forensics systematically track and analyze outcomes for accountability and quality

improvement?
<--- Score

98. Where is it measured?
<--- Score

99. How do you focus on what is right -not who is right?
<--- Score

100. Who participated in the data collection for measurements?
<--- Score

101. Is it possible to estimate the impact of unanticipated complexity such as wrong or failed assumptions, feedback, etc. on proposed reforms?
<--- Score

102. What are the types and number of measures to use?
<--- Score

103. What measurements are possible, practicable and meaningful?
<--- Score

104. Have you found any 'ground fruit' or 'low-hanging fruit' for immediate remedies to the gap in performance?
<--- Score

105. Have all non-recommended alternatives been analyzed in sufficient detail?
<--- Score

106. Was a data collection plan established?
<--- Score

107. Is the solution cost-effective?
<--- Score

108. What file systems can the tool analyze?
<--- Score

109. Do you aggressively reward and promote the people who have the biggest impact on creating excellent Digital Forensics services/products?
<--- Score

110. How do you know that any Digital Forensics analysis is complete and comprehensive?
<--- Score

111. What causes investor action?
<--- Score

112. Given the time-sensitive nature, how should analysts prioritize actions?
<--- Score

Add up total points for this section:
_ _ _ _ _ = Total points for this section

Divided by: _ _ _ _ _ _ (number of statements answered) = _ _ _ _ _ _
Average score for this section

Transfer your score to the Digital Forensics Index at the beginning of the Self-Assessment.

CRITERION #4: ANALYZE:

INTENT: Analyze causes, assumptions and hypotheses.

In my belief, the answer to this question is clearly defined:

5 Strongly Agree

4 Agree

3 Neutral

2 Disagree

1 Strongly Disagree

1. What did the team gain from developing a sub-process map?
<--- Score

2. What methods do you use to gather Digital Forensics data?
<--- Score

3. An organizationally feasible system request is one that considers the mission, goals and objectives of

the organization. Key questions are: is the Digital Forensics solution request practical and will it solve a problem or take advantage of an opportunity to achieve company goals?

<--- Score

4. What are your key performance measures or indicators and in-process measures for the control and improvement of your Digital Forensics processes?

<--- Score

5. How was the detailed process map generated, verified, and validated?

<--- Score

6. Do your employees have the opportunity to do what they do best everyday?

<--- Score

7. What are your current levels and trends in key Digital Forensics measures or indicators of product and process performance that are important to and directly serve your customers?

<--- Score

8. Are gaps between current performance and the goal performance identified?

<--- Score

9. How do your work systems and key work processes relate to and capitalize on your core competencies?

<--- Score

10. Were there any improvement opportunities identified from the process analysis?

<--- Score

11. How is the way you as the leader think and process information affecting your organizational culture?
<--- Score

12. Can cyber security event data be transmitted securely for digital forensics by the appropriate entities (e.g., manufacturer, vendor, law enforcement)?
<--- Score

13. How do you use Digital Forensics data and information to support organizational decision making and innovation?
<--- Score

14. How does the organization define, manage, and improve its Digital Forensics processes?
<--- Score

15. How do mission and objectives affect the Digital Forensics processes of your organization?
<--- Score

16. Record-keeping requirements flow from the records needed as inputs, outputs, controls and for transformation of a Digital Forensics process. Are the records needed as inputs to the Digital Forensics process available?
<--- Score

17. Did any additional data need to be collected?
<--- Score

18. What data is gathered?
<--- Score

19. Do your contracts/agreements contain data security obligations?
<--- Score

20. What does the data say about the performance of the business process?
<--- Score

21. How much data do you save?
<--- Score

22. What is the cost of poor quality as supported by the team's analysis?
<--- Score

23. Were Pareto charts (or similar) used to portray the 'heavy hitters' (or key sources of variation)?
<--- Score

24. Do several people in different organizational units assist with the Digital Forensics process?
<--- Score

25. Where is Digital Forensics data gathered?
<--- Score

26. Which data source would be checked first and why?
<--- Score

27. What data should you capture?
<--- Score

28. What tools were used to narrow the list of possible causes?

<--- Score

29. Was a detailed process map created to amplify critical steps of the 'as is' business process?
<--- Score

30. What conclusions were drawn from the team's data collection and analysis? How did the team reach these conclusions?
<--- Score

31. How do you implement and manage your work processes to ensure that they meet design requirements?
<--- Score

32. Have the problem and goal statements been updated to reflect the additional knowledge gained from the analyze phase?
<--- Score

33. Think about the functions involved in your Digital Forensics project, what processes flow from these functions?
<--- Score

34. What are the best opportunities for value improvement?
<--- Score

35. Is Data and process analysis, root cause analysis and quantifying the gap/opportunity in place?
<--- Score

36. What are your current levels and trends in key measures or indicators of Digital Forensics product

and process performance that are important to and directly serve your customers? How do these results compare with the performance of your competitors and other organizations with similar offerings?
<--- Score

37. Is the required Digital Forensics data gathered?
<--- Score

38. What data should be collected?
<--- Score

39. How do you promote understanding that opportunity for improvement is not criticism of the status quo, or the people who created the status quo?
<--- Score

40. What were the financial benefits resulting from any 'ground fruit or low-hanging fruit' (quick fixes)?
<--- Score

41. What quality tools were used to get through the analyze phase?
<--- Score

42. Do your leaders quickly bounce back from setbacks?
<--- Score

43. What data to save?
<--- Score

44. Is relevant cyber security event data captured for purposes of digital forensics?
<--- Score

45. Was a cause-and-effect diagram used to explore the different types of causes (or sources of variation)?
<--- Score

46. What are the potential sources of data?
<--- Score

47. What is your organizations process which leads to recognition of value generation?
<--- Score

48. What Digital Forensics data do you gather or use now?
<--- Score

49. What other jobs or tasks affect the performance of the steps in the Digital Forensics process?
<--- Score

50. Who should determine how much effort should be put into attempting to recover encrypted data?
<--- Score

51. Have any additional benefits been identified that will result from closing all or most of the gaps?
<--- Score

52. Is the gap/opportunity displayed and communicated in financial terms?
<--- Score

53. How often will data be collected for measures?
<--- Score

54. What are the most likely possible data sources outside of the users office?

<--- Score

55. How is Digital Forensics data gathered?
<--- Score

56. Think about some of the processes you undertake within your organization, which do you own?
<--- Score

57. What are your best practices for minimizing Digital Forensics project risk, while demonstrating incremental value and quick wins throughout the Digital Forensics project lifecycle?
<--- Score

58. Of the potential sources of data, which are the most likely to contain helpful information and why?
<--- Score

59. What process should you select for improvement?
<--- Score

60. Is the suppliers process defined and controlled?
<--- Score

61. What other organizational variables, such as reward systems or communication systems, affect the performance of this Digital Forensics process?
<--- Score

62. A compounding model resolution with available relevant data can often provide insight towards a solution methodology; which Digital Forensics models, tools and techniques are necessary?
<--- Score

63. What were the crucial 'moments of truth' on the process map?
<--- Score

64. Did any value-added analysis or 'lean thinking' take place to identify some of the gaps shown on the 'as is' process map?
<--- Score

65. How do you identify specific Digital Forensics investment opportunities and emerging trends?
<--- Score

66. What tools were used to generate the list of possible causes?
<--- Score

67. Is the Digital Forensics process severely broken such that a re-design is necessary?
<--- Score

68. Are Digital Forensics changes recognized early enough to be approved through the regular process?
<--- Score

69. How would the use of forensic tools and techniques change if the infected desktop systems were used to process sensitive information that the organization is required to safeguard?
<--- Score

70. Do you, as a leader, bounce back quickly from setbacks?
<--- Score

71. What controls do you have in place to protect data?
<--- Score

72. What are your Digital Forensics processes?
<--- Score

73. Were any designed experiments used to generate additional insight into the data analysis?
<--- Score

74. Identify an operational issue in your organization. for example, could a particular task be done more quickly or more efficiently by Digital Forensics?
<--- Score

75. What successful thing are you doing today that may be blinding you to new growth opportunities?
<--- Score

76. What are the revised rough estimates of the financial savings/opportunity for Digital Forensics improvements?
<--- Score

77. Is the performance gap determined?
<--- Score

78. Can you add value to the current Digital Forensics decision-making process (largely qualitative) by incorporating uncertainty modeling (more quantitative)?
<--- Score

79. How do you measure the operational performance of your key work systems and processes, including

productivity, cycle time, and other appropriate measures of process effectiveness, efficiency, and innovation?
<--- Score

80. Where is the data coming from to measure compliance?
<--- Score

Add up total points for this section:
_ _ _ _ _ = Total points for this section

Divided by: _ _ _ _ _ _ (number of statements answered) = _ _ _ _ _ _
Average score for this section

Transfer your score to the Digital Forensics Index at the beginning of the Self-Assessment.

CRITERION #5: IMPROVE:

INTENT: Develop a practical solution. Innovate, establish and test the solution and to measure the results.

In my belief, the answer to this question is clearly defined:

5 Strongly Agree

4 Agree

3 Neutral

2 Disagree

1 Strongly Disagree

1. How do you improve Digital Forensics service perception, and satisfaction?
<--- Score

2. Who are the people involved in developing and implementing Digital Forensics?
<--- Score

3. What practices helps your organization to develop

its capacity to recognize patterns?
<--- Score

4. What improvements have been achieved?
<--- Score

5. What lessons, if any, from a pilot were incorporated into the design of the full-scale solution?
<--- Score

6. Are new and improved process ('should be') maps developed?
<--- Score

7. Is the measure of success for Digital Forensics understandable to a variety of people?
<--- Score

8. What are the implications of the one critical Digital Forensics decision 10 minutes, 10 months, and 10 years from now?
<--- Score

9. Are improved process ('should be') maps modified based on pilot data and analysis?
<--- Score

10. How will you know that a change is an improvement?
<--- Score

11. Is pilot data collected and analyzed?
<--- Score

12. Is there a high likelihood that any recommendations will achieve their intended results?

<--- Score

13. Do those selected for the Digital Forensics team have a good general understanding of what Digital Forensics is all about?
<--- Score

14. How can you improve performance?
<--- Score

15. How do you manage and improve your Digital Forensics work systems to deliver customer value and achieve organizational success and sustainability?
<--- Score

16. What were the underlying assumptions on the cost-benefit analysis?
<--- Score

17. Is supporting Digital Forensics documentation required?
<--- Score

18. For decision problems, how do you develop a decision statement?
<--- Score

19. What do you want to improve?
<--- Score

20. How do you define the solutions' scope?
<--- Score

21. Is the optimal solution selected based on testing and analysis?
<--- Score

22. Is a contingency plan established?
<--- Score

23. Is the implementation plan designed?
<--- Score

24. How do you improve your likelihood of success ?
<--- Score

25. What is the Digital Forensics's sustainability risk?
<--- Score

26. How are the results handled?
<--- Score

27. What is Digital Forensics's impact on utilizing the best solution(s)?
<--- Score

28. What is the magnitude of the improvements?
<--- Score

29. What is the team's contingency plan for potential problems occurring in implementation?
<--- Score

30. How do you improve productivity?
<--- Score

31. Why improve in the first place?
<--- Score

32. How does the team improve its work?
<--- Score

33. Are the best solutions selected?
<--- Score

34. How do you measure risk?
<--- Score

35. What went well, what should change, what can improve?
<--- Score

36. What needs improvement? Why?
<--- Score

37. Are you assessing Digital Forensics and risk?
<--- Score

38. Does the goal represent a desired result that can be measured?
<--- Score

39. Risk factors: what are the characteristics of Digital Forensics that make it risky?
<--- Score

40. Was a pilot designed for the proposed solution(s)?
<--- Score

41. How do the Digital Forensics results compare with the performance of your competitors and other organizations with similar offerings?
<--- Score

42. How can you improve Digital Forensics?
<--- Score

43. What tools were used to tap into the creativity and

encourage 'outside the box' thinking?
<--- Score

44. Is there a small-scale pilot for proposed improvement(s)? What conclusions were drawn from the outcomes of a pilot?
<--- Score

45. Will the controls trigger any other risks?
<--- Score

46. In the past few months, what is the smallest change you have made that has had the biggest positive result? What was it about that small change that produced the large return?
<--- Score

47. Is the scope clearly documented?
<--- Score

48. Who will be responsible for making the decisions to include or exclude requested changes once Digital Forensics is underway?
<--- Score

49. Describe the design of the pilot and what tests were conducted, if any?
<--- Score

50. What communications are necessary to support the implementation of the solution?
<--- Score

51. Risk Identification: What are the possible risk events your organization faces in relation to Digital Forensics?

<--- Score

52. To what extent does management recognize Digital Forensics as a tool to increase the results?
<--- Score

53. Who controls key decisions that will be made?
<--- Score

54. How did the team generate the list of possible solutions?
<--- Score

55. What to do with the results or outcomes of measurements?
<--- Score

56. How do you keep improving Digital Forensics?
<--- Score

57. How will you know when its improved?
<--- Score

58. Risk events: what are the things that could go wrong?
<--- Score

59. How would forensic tools and techniques be used if application developers were confident that an operational problem was causing the issues?
<--- Score

60. How will you measure the results?
<--- Score

61. Who controls the risk?

<--- Score

62. What tools were used to evaluate the potential solutions?
<--- Score

63. How do you measure progress and evaluate training effectiveness?
<--- Score

64. How can skill-level changes improve Digital Forensics?
<--- Score

65. If you could go back in time five years, what decision would you make differently? What is your best guess as to what decision you're making today you might regret five years from now?
<--- Score

66. What does the 'should be' process map/design look like?
<--- Score

67. Can the solution be designed and implemented within an acceptable time period?
<--- Score

68. Explorations of the frontiers of Digital Forensics will help you build influence, improve Digital Forensics, optimize decision making, and sustain change, what is your approach?
<--- Score

69. How do you go about comparing Digital Forensics approaches/solutions?

<--- Score

70. How do you measure improved Digital Forensics service perception, and satisfaction?
<--- Score

71. Dynamic: what system states do you document when there is an intrusion?
<--- Score

72. How will you know that you have improved?
<--- Score

73. Are there any constraints (technical, political, cultural, or otherwise) that would inhibit certain solutions?
<--- Score

74. What are your current levels and trends in key measures or indicators of workforce and leader development?
<--- Score

75. Are possible solutions generated and tested?
<--- Score

76. How will the organization know that the solution worked?
<--- Score

77. Who will be responsible for documenting the Digital Forensics requirements in detail?
<--- Score

78. What tools were most useful during the improve phase?

<--- Score

79. What attendant changes will need to be made to ensure that the solution is successful?
<--- Score

80. Can you identify any significant risks or exposures to Digital Forensics third- parties (vendors, service providers, alliance partners etc) that concern you?
<--- Score

81. What actually has to improve and by how much?
<--- Score

82. How will the team or the process owner(s) monitor the implementation plan to see that it is working as intended?
<--- Score

83. Which of the recognised risks out of all risks can be most likely transferred?
<--- Score

84. What error proofing will be done to address some of the discrepancies observed in the 'as is' process?
<--- Score

85. How do you link measurement and risk?
<--- Score

86. For estimation problems, how do you develop an estimation statement?
<--- Score

87. Are risk triggers captured?
<--- Score

88. How significant is the improvement in the eyes of the end user?
<--- Score

89. What can you do to improve?
<--- Score

90. What is the risk?
<--- Score

91. Is the solution technically practical?
<--- Score

92. Relevant and/or Material: How do you know if information assists decision-makers in tasks?
<--- Score

93. Is a solution implementation plan established, including schedule/work breakdown structure, resources, risk management plan, cost/budget, and control plan?
<--- Score

94. Who will be using the results of the measurement activities?
<--- Score

95. Were any criteria developed to assist the team in testing and evaluating potential solutions?
<--- Score

96. What current systems have to be understood and/or changed?
<--- Score

97. How does the solution remove the key sources of issues discovered in the analyze phase?
<--- Score

98. What resources are required for the improvement efforts?
<--- Score

99. What is the implementation plan?
<--- Score

100. Is there a cost/benefit analysis of optimal solution(s)?
<--- Score

Add up total points for this section:
_ _ _ _ _ = Total points for this section

Divided by: _ _ _ _ _ _ (number of statements answered) = _ _ _ _ _ _
Average score for this section

Transfer your score to the Digital Forensics Index at the beginning of the Self-Assessment.

CRITERION #6: CONTROL:

INTENT: Implement the practical solution. Maintain the performance and correct possible complications.

In my belief, the answer to this question is clearly defined:

5 Strongly Agree

4 Agree

3 Neutral

2 Disagree

1 Strongly Disagree

1. Does the Digital Forensics performance meet the customer's requirements?
<--- Score

2. Does a troubleshooting guide exist or is it needed?
<--- Score

3. Is there a transfer of ownership and knowledge to process owner and process team tasked with the

responsibilities.
<--- Score

4. Will any special training be provided for results interpretation?
<--- Score

5. Does the response plan contain a definite closed loop continual improvement scheme (e.g., plan-do-check-act)?
<--- Score

6. How will report readings be checked to effectively monitor performance?
<--- Score

7. What are the key elements of your Digital Forensics performance improvement system, including your evaluation, organizational learning, and innovation processes?
<--- Score

8. What adjustments to the strategies are needed?
<--- Score

9. What other areas of the organization might benefit from the Digital Forensics team's improvements, knowledge, and learning?
<--- Score

10. Is there a standardized process?
<--- Score

11. How will the day-to-day responsibilities for monitoring and continual improvement be transferred from the improvement team to the

process owner?
<--- Score

12. Is new knowledge gained imbedded in the response plan?
<--- Score

13. Does job training on the documented procedures need to be part of the process team's education and training?
<--- Score

14. Are new process steps, standards, and documentation ingrained into normal operations?
<--- Score

15. You may have created your quality measures at a time when you lacked resources, technology wasn't up to the required standard, or low service levels were the industry norm. Have those circumstances changed?
<--- Score

16. Is a response plan established and deployed?
<--- Score

17. Is there documentation that will support the successful operation of the improvement?
<--- Score

18. How will input, process, and output variables be checked to detect for sub-optimal conditions?
<--- Score

19. How do you establish and deploy modified action plans if circumstances require a shift in plans and

rapid execution of new plans?

<--- Score

20. What should the next improvement project be that is related to Digital Forensics?

<--- Score

21. How do your controls stack up?

<--- Score

22. How do senior leaders actions reflect a commitment to the organizations Digital Forensics values?

<--- Score

23. In the case of a Digital Forensics project, the criteria for the audit derive from implementation objectives. an audit of a Digital Forensics project involves assessing whether the recommendations outlined for implementation have been met. Can you track that any Digital Forensics project is implemented as planned, and is it working?

<--- Score

24. Can you adapt and adjust to changing Digital Forensics situations?

<--- Score

25. Implementation Planning: is a pilot needed to test the changes before a full roll out occurs?

<--- Score

26. Do you monitor the effectiveness of your Digital Forensics activities?

<--- Score

27. Who sets the Digital Forensics standards?
<--- Score

28. Are the planned controls in place?
<--- Score

29. Are the planned controls working?
<--- Score

30. How do you select, collect, align, and integrate Digital Forensics data and information for tracking daily operations and overall organizational performance, including progress relative to strategic objectives and action plans?
<--- Score

31. What are you attempting to measure/monitor?
<--- Score

32. Do the Digital Forensics decisions you make today help people and the planet tomorrow?
<--- Score

33. What should you measure to verify efficiency gains?
<--- Score

34. Can support from partners be adjusted?
<--- Score

35. How do controls support value?
<--- Score

36. How will new or emerging customer needs/ requirements be checked/communicated to orient the process toward meeting the new specifications

and continually reducing variation?
<--- Score

37. Are pertinent alerts monitored, analyzed and distributed to appropriate personnel?
<--- Score

38. What quality tools were useful in the control phase?
<--- Score

39. Who controls critical resources?
<--- Score

40. Act/Adjust: What Do you Need to Do Differently?
<--- Score

41. Are there documented procedures?
<--- Score

42. Has the improved process and its steps been standardized?
<--- Score

43. Does Digital Forensics appropriately measure and monitor risk?
<--- Score

44. Do you monitor the Digital Forensics decisions made and fine tune them as they evolve?
<--- Score

45. Are controls in place and consistently applied?
<--- Score

46. Have new or revised work instructions resulted?

<--- Score

47. Is there a Digital Forensics Communication plan covering who needs to get what information when?
<--- Score

48. What is your theory of human motivation, and how does your compensation plan fit with that view?
<--- Score

49. What is the recommended frequency of auditing?
<--- Score

50. Is there a recommended audit plan for routine surveillance inspections of Digital Forensics's gains?
<--- Score

51. Is there a documented and implemented monitoring plan?
<--- Score

52. Who has control over resources?
<--- Score

53. How will the process owner verify improvement in present and future sigma levels, process capabilities?
<--- Score

54. Are suggested corrective/restorative actions indicated on the response plan for known causes to problems that might surface?
<--- Score

55. How will the process owner and team be able to hold the gains?
<--- Score

56. Is reporting being used or needed?
<--- Score

57. How will you measure your QA plan's effectiveness?
<--- Score

58. Will your goals reflect your program budget?
<--- Score

59. Will the team be available to assist members in planning investigations?
<--- Score

60. Are you measuring, monitoring and predicting Digital Forensics activities to optimize operations and profitability, and enhancing outcomes?
<--- Score

61. How might the organization capture best practices and lessons learned so as to leverage improvements across the business?
<--- Score

62. What do you measure to verify effectiveness gains?
<--- Score

63. What key inputs and outputs are being measured on an ongoing basis?
<--- Score

64. What do your reports reflect?
<--- Score

65. What other systems, operations, processes, and infrastructures (hiring practices, staffing, training, incentives/rewards, metrics/dashboards/scorecards, etc.) need updates, additions, changes, or deletions in order to facilitate knowledge transfer and improvements?
<--- Score

66. What do you stand for--and what are you against?
<--- Score

67. What are the critical parameters to watch?
<--- Score

68. What is the best design framework for Digital Forensics organization now that, in a post industrial-age if the top-down, command and control model is no longer relevant?
<--- Score

69. Where do ideas that reach policy makers and planners as proposals for Digital Forensics strengthening and reform actually originate?
<--- Score

70. Is a response plan in place for when the input, process, or output measures indicate an 'out-of-control' condition?
<--- Score

71. Are documented procedures clear and easy to follow for the operators?
<--- Score

72. Who will be in control?
<--- Score

73. How do you encourage people to take control and responsibility?
<--- Score

74. Who is the Digital Forensics process owner?
<--- Score

75. How is change control managed?
<--- Score

76. How likely is the current Digital Forensics plan to come in on schedule or on budget?
<--- Score

77. Is there a control plan in place for sustaining improvements (short and long-term)?
<--- Score

78. How can you best use all of your knowledge repositories to enhance learning and sharing?
<--- Score

79. What can you control?
<--- Score

80. What are the known security controls?
<--- Score

81. Are operating procedures consistent?
<--- Score

82. How do you plan on providing proper recognition and disclosure of supporting companies?
<--- Score

83. Against what alternative is success being measured?
<--- Score

84. Is knowledge gained on process shared and institutionalized?
<--- Score

85. What is the control/monitoring plan?
<--- Score

Add up total points for this section:
_____ = Total points for this section

Divided by: _____ (number of statements answered) = _____
Average score for this section

Transfer your score to the Digital Forensics Index at the beginning of the Self-Assessment.

CRITERION #7: SUSTAIN:

INTENT: Retain the benefits.

In my belief, the answer to this question is clearly defined:

5 Strongly Agree

4 Agree

3 Neutral

2 Disagree

1 Strongly Disagree

1. What business benefits will Digital Forensics goals deliver if achieved?
<--- Score

2. How will you insure seamless interoperability of Digital Forensics moving forward?
<--- Score

3. What is the source of the strategies for Digital Forensics strengthening and reform?
<--- Score

4. What new services of functionality will be implemented next with Digital Forensics ?
<--- Score

5. Is Digital Forensics dependent on the successful delivery of a current project?
<--- Score

6. How do you know if you are successful?
<--- Score

7. What is effective Digital Forensics?
<--- Score

8. What is something you believe that nearly no one agrees with you on?
<--- Score

9. What will be the consequences to the stakeholder (financial, reputation etc) if Digital Forensics does not go ahead or fails to deliver the objectives?
<--- Score

10. How do you govern and fulfill your societal responsibilities?
<--- Score

11. If you had to leave your organization for a year and the only communication you could have with employees/colleagues was a single paragraph, what would you write?
<--- Score

12. Who performs the investigation and under what circumstances?

<--- Score

13. What is an unauthorized commitment?
<--- Score

14. If you weren't already in this business, would you enter it today? And if not, what are you going to do about it?
<--- Score

15. What are the challenges?
<--- Score

16. How can you incorporate support to ensure safe and effective use of Digital Forensics into the services that you provide?
<--- Score

17. How would the forensic activity change if the DDoS attack appeared to be coming from a network in a different state?
<--- Score

18. How do you maintain Digital Forensics's Integrity?
<--- Score

19. Who is responsible for ensuring appropriate resources (time, people and money) are allocated to Digital Forensics?
<--- Score

20. Which witnesses should be called?
<--- Score

21. Is the impact that Digital Forensics has shown?
<--- Score

22. How do you transition from the baseline to the target?
<--- Score

23. Do you have enough freaky customers in your portfolio pushing you to the limit day in and day out?
<--- Score

24. Do you have past Digital Forensics successes?
<--- Score

25. Are all key stakeholders present at all Structured Walkthroughs?
<--- Score

26. How do customers see your organization?
<--- Score

27. Whose voice (department, ethnic group, women, older workers, etc) might you have missed hearing from in your company, and how might you amplify this voice to create positive momentum for your business?
<--- Score

28. How do you listen to customers to obtain actionable information?
<--- Score

29. Marketing budgets are tighter, consumers are more skeptical, and social media has changed forever the way we talk about Digital Forensics. How do you gain traction?
<--- Score

30. What are the key enablers to make this Digital Forensics move?

<--- Score

31. Is maximizing Digital Forensics protection the same as minimizing Digital Forensics loss?

<--- Score

32. What one word do you want to own in the minds of your customers, employees, and partners?

<--- Score

33. Is a Digital Forensics team work effort in place?

<--- Score

34. What would have to be true for the option on the table to be the best possible choice?

<--- Score

35. Where should be the place of litigation?

<--- Score

36. What types of forensic tools are used to locate the access point overtly?

<--- Score

37. How much does Digital Forensics help?

<--- Score

38. Can you break it down?

<--- Score

39. What are the toughest challenges your organization faces with regards to digital evidence?

<--- Score

40. Who do you think the world wants your organization to be?
<--- Score

41. Is there any reason to believe the opposite of my current belief?
<--- Score

42. Which piece of evidence is relevant and admissible?
<--- Score

43. What happens at your organization when people fail?
<--- Score

44. How do you lead with Digital Forensics in mind?
<--- Score

45. Which litigation mechanism should be used?
<--- Score

46. Think of your Digital Forensics project, what are the main functions?
<--- Score

47. What happens if you do not have enough funding?
<--- Score

48. If your customer were your grandmother, would you tell her to buy what you're selling?
<--- Score

49. What are current Digital Forensics paradigms?

<--- Score

50. What must you excel at?
<--- Score

51. How can this help law enforcement?
<--- Score

52. Have new benefits been realized?
<--- Score

53. Is it economical; do you have the time and money?
<--- Score

54. How might privacy considerations affect the use of forensic tools and techniques?
<--- Score

55. How should the technical and non-technical aspects of an investigation be coordinated and balanced?
<--- Score

56. How are you doing compared to your industry?
<--- Score

57. How do you accomplish your long range Digital Forensics goals?
<--- Score

58. Who will provide the final approval of Digital Forensics deliverables?
<--- Score

59. What did you miss in the interview for the worst hire you ever made?

<--- Score

60. What does your signature ensure?
<--- Score

61. Attacker threat level: Does the attacker represent a great threat?
<--- Score

62. How do you ensure that implementations of Digital Forensics products are done in a way that ensures safety?
<--- Score

63. What is the craziest thing you can do?
<--- Score

64. Which models, tools and techniques are necessary?
<--- Score

65. How long will it take to change?
<--- Score

66. Do you have the right people on the bus?
<--- Score

67. What management system can you use to leverage the Digital Forensics experience, ideas, and concerns of the people closest to the work to be done?
<--- Score

68. How do you determine the key elements that affect Digital Forensics workforce satisfaction, how are these elements determined for different workforce

groups and segments?
<--- Score

69. What are the rules and assumptions your industry operates under? What if the opposite were true?
<--- Score

70. How is an investigation handled across departments?
<--- Score

71. What privacy concerns should be considered in investigating employees financial transactions?
<--- Score

72. How does Digital Forensics integrate with other business initiatives?
<--- Score

73. How will you know that the Digital Forensics project has been successful?
<--- Score

74. In retrospect, of the projects that you pulled the plug on, what percent do you wish had been allowed to keep going, and what percent do you wish had ended earlier?
<--- Score

75. What are the short and long-term Digital Forensics goals?
<--- Score

76. Why will customers want to buy your organizations products/services?
<--- Score

77. Were lessons learned captured and communicated?
<--- Score

78. What Digital Forensics skills are most important?
<--- Score

79. How can you trust audit trails?
<--- Score

80. Is it consistent with the models in the field of Digital Forensics?
<--- Score

81. Have benefits been optimized with all key stakeholders?
<--- Score

82. What are the long-term Digital Forensics goals?
<--- Score

83. In a project to restructure Digital Forensics outcomes, which stakeholders would you involve?
<--- Score

84. How do you assess the Digital Forensics pitfalls that are inherent in implementing it?
<--- Score

85. What will drive Digital Forensics change?
<--- Score

86. How do you decide how much to remunerate an employee?
<--- Score

87. Are the criteria for selecting recommendations stated?
<--- Score

88. How can you become the company that would put you out of business?
<--- Score

89. What is the vendors reputation for providing support?
<--- Score

90. Who will be responsible for deciding whether Digital Forensics goes ahead or not after the initial investigations?
<--- Score

91. What is your BATNA (best alternative to a negotiated agreement)?
<--- Score

92. Did your employees make progress today?
<--- Score

93. Why not do Digital Forensics?
<--- Score

94. One of the key features of the scientific method is testing, but what constitutes a test?
<--- Score

95. Is your basic point _____ or _____?
<--- Score

96. What are the success criteria that will indicate that

Digital Forensics objectives have been met and the benefits delivered?

<--- Score

97. What is your competitive advantage?

<--- Score

98. Are there any activities that you can take off your to do list?

<--- Score

99. How do you create buy-in?

<--- Score

100. Why is it important to have senior management support for a Digital Forensics project?

<--- Score

101. At what moment would you think; Will I get fired?

<--- Score

102. What Digital Forensics modifications can you make work for you?

<--- Score

103. Do you feel that more should be done in the Digital Forensics area?

<--- Score

104. If you were responsible for initiating and implementing major changes in your organization, what steps might you take to ensure acceptance of those changes?

<--- Score

105. What is the funding source for this project?

<--- Score

106. Are your responses positive or negative?
<--- Score

107. Are there any disadvantages to implementing Digital Forensics? There might be some that are less obvious?
<--- Score

108. What are your most important goals for the strategic Digital Forensics objectives?
<--- Score

109. What is/are the relevant law/ordinance?
<--- Score

110. What are internal and external Digital Forensics relations?
<--- Score

111. Do Digital Forensics rules make a reasonable demand on a users capabilities?
<--- Score

112. What counts that you are not counting?
<--- Score

113. Are you relevant? Will you be relevant five years from now? Ten?
<--- Score

114. How can you become more high-tech but still be high touch?
<--- Score

115. What are specific Digital Forensics rules to follow?
<--- Score

116. How would the forensic activity change if a DDoS attack appeared to be coming from a business partners network?
<--- Score

117. Is there a work around that you can use?
<--- Score

118. Political -is anyone trying to undermine this project?
<--- Score

119. How do you think fictional crime dramas have affected the public perception of forensic science?
<--- Score

120. Biometrics Resources: What is academia doing?
<--- Score

121. How would the forensic activity change if a DDoS attack appeared to be coming from a network in a different state?
<--- Score

122. What threat is Digital Forensics addressing?
<--- Score

123. Can you maintain your growth without detracting from the factors that have contributed to your success?
<--- Score

124. How would the forensic activities change if it was determined that an unknown individual had been seen deploying an access point?

<--- Score

125. Should the expert witness and the forencis specialist be one and the same?

<--- Score

126. Who do you want your customers to become?

<--- Score

127. What information is critical to your organization that your executives are ignoring?

<--- Score

128. What trouble can you get into?

<--- Score

129. Why should people listen to you?

<--- Score

130. Do you say no to customers for no reason?

<--- Score

131. What are strategies for increasing support and reducing opposition?

<--- Score

132. Are you paying enough attention to the partners your company depends on to succeed?

<--- Score

133. If there were zero limitations, what would you do differently?

<--- Score

134. How do you keep records, of what?
<--- Score

135. What evidence should be presented?
<--- Score

136. Who will determine interim and final deadlines?
<--- Score

137. What is the estimated value of the project?
<--- Score

138. What litigation scheme should be used?
<--- Score

139. How do you keep the momentum going?
<--- Score

140. Legal constraints: Must the incident be communicated to the police?
<--- Score

141. Why do and why don't your customers like your organization?
<--- Score

142. Is sufficient evidence collected?
<--- Score

143. How can you negotiate Digital Forensics successfully with a stubborn boss, an irate client, or a deceitful coworker?
<--- Score

144. Which groups and individuals within your

**organization would probably be involved in the
forensic activities?**

<--- Score

145. Which functions and people interact with the supplier and or customer?

<--- Score

146. How do you set Digital Forensics stretch targets and how do you get people to not only participate in setting these stretch targets but also that they strive to achieve these?

<--- Score

147. Digital Forensics: What are you looking for?

<--- Score

148. How would the forensic activities change if it was determined that an unknown individual had been seen deploying the access point?

<--- Score

149. What is your question? Why?

<--- Score

150. Who are your customers?

<--- Score

151. What projects are going on in the organization today, and what resources are those projects using from the resource pools?

<--- Score

152. What goals did you miss?

<--- Score

153. What relationships among Digital Forensics trends do you perceive?
<--- Score

154. How do you proactively clarify deliverables and Digital Forensics quality expectations?
<--- Score

155. Operational - will it work?
<--- Score

156. Are assumptions made in Digital Forensics stated explicitly?
<--- Score

157. Where can you break convention?
<--- Score

158. What types of forensic tools are used to locate an access point overtly?
<--- Score

159. Who have you, as a company, historically been when you've been at your best?
<--- Score

160. How do you foster innovation?
<--- Score

161. How do you provide a safe environment -physically and emotionally?
<--- Score

162. How would the forensic activities change if it was determined that the access point was deployed for a legitimate business purpose, such

as temporary work at the office by a contractor?
<--- Score

163. How do you deal with Digital Forensics changes?
<--- Score

164. To whom do you add value?
<--- Score

165. Why should you adopt a Digital Forensics framework?
<--- Score

166. What are the potential basics of Digital Forensics fraud?
<--- Score

167. Who do we want your customers to become?
<--- Score

168. Has implementation been effective in reaching specified objectives so far?
<--- Score

169. Will it be accepted by users?
<--- Score

170. Who are the key stakeholders?
<--- Score

171. What have you done to protect your business from competitive encroachment?
<--- Score

172. Do you think you know, or do you know you know ?

<--- Score

173. What is a feasible sequencing of reform initiatives over time?
<--- Score

174. Which Digital Forensics goals are the most important?
<--- Score

175. Are you / should you be revolutionary or evolutionary?
<--- Score

176. What do we do when new problems arise?
<--- Score

177. Should you Quarantine?
<--- Score

178. What is the range of capabilities?
<--- Score

179. If your company went out of business tomorrow, would anyone who doesn't get a paycheck here care?
<--- Score

180. If no one would ever find out about your accomplishments, how would you lead differently?
<--- Score

181. Are you satisfied with your current role? If not, what is missing from it?
<--- Score

182. What stupid rule would you most like to kill?

<--- Score

183. What are the gaps in your knowledge and experience?
<--- Score

184. How will you motivate the stakeholders with the least vested interest?
<--- Score

185. What is the purpose of Digital Forensics in relation to the mission?
<--- Score

186. What should you stop doing?
<--- Score

187. What is the recommended frequency of auditing?
<--- Score

188. What connectivity does the network or system have to other areas in the organization?
<--- Score

189. How do you track customer value, profitability or financial return, organizational success, and sustainability?
<--- Score

190. What are you challenging?
<--- Score

191. Would you rather sell to knowledgeable and informed customers or to uninformed customers?
<--- Score

192. What circumstances warrant investigation?

<--- Score

193. What is the kind of project structure that would be appropriate for your Digital Forensics project, should it be formal and complex, or can it be less formal and relatively simple?

<--- Score

194. How do you foster the skills, knowledge, talents, attributes, and characteristics you want to have?

<--- Score

195. Potential damage: Is the expected damage large?

<--- Score

196. Which individuals, teams or departments will be involved in Digital Forensics?

<--- Score

197. How likely is it that a customer would recommend your company to a friend or colleague?

<--- Score

198. How would the forensic activity change if the DDoS attack appeared to be coming from a business partner's network?

<--- Score

199. What are the barriers to increased Digital Forensics production?

<--- Score

200. How would the use of forensic tools and techniques change if a worm disrupted network

communications?

<--- Score

201. If you got fired and a new hire took your place, what would she do different?

<--- Score

202. Which groups and individuals within the organization would probably be involved in the forensic activities?

<--- Score

203. Whom among your colleagues do you trust, and for what?

<--- Score

204. Instead of going to current contacts for new ideas, what if you reconnected with dormant contacts--the people you used to know? If you were going reactivate a dormant tie, who would it be?

<--- Score

205. Who uses your product in ways you never expected?

<--- Score

206. What tactic should be applied in a litigation procedure?

<--- Score

207. Can the schedule be done in the given time?

<--- Score

208. How important is Digital Forensics to the user organizations mission?

<--- Score

209. In the past year, what have you done (or could you have done) to increase the accurate perception of your company/brand as ethical and honest?
<--- Score

210. Is the Digital Forensics organization completing tasks effectively and efficiently?
<--- Score

211. How do you make it meaningful in connecting Digital Forensics with what users do day-to-day?
<--- Score

212. Who will manage the integration of tools?
<--- Score

213. When you map the key players in your own work and the types/domains of relationships with them, which relationships do you find easy and which challenging, and why?
<--- Score

214. What may be the consequences for the performance of an organization if all stakeholders are not consulted regarding Digital Forensics?
<--- Score

215. Ask yourself: how would you do this work if you only had one staff member to do it?
<--- Score

216. How do you go about securing Digital Forensics?
<--- Score

217. What are the business goals Digital Forensics is

aiming to achieve?
<--- Score

218. What are you trying to prove to yourself, and how might it be hijacking your life and business success?
<--- Score

219. What role does communication play in the success or failure of a Digital Forensics project?
<--- Score

220. Can a scripting language be used with the tool to automate repetitive functions?
<--- Score

221. Are you changing as fast as the world around you?
<--- Score

222. Should any expert witnesses be called?
<--- Score

223. What would you recommend your friend do if he/she were facing this dilemma?
<--- Score

224. Response posture: Does the organization follow a zero tolerance policy?
<--- Score

225. What is it like to work for you?
<--- Score

226. Are new benefits received and understood?
<--- Score

227. What unique value proposition (UVP) do you offer?
<--- Score

228. How is implementation research currently incorporated into each of your goals?
<--- Score

229. Who is responsible for errors?
<--- Score

230. What was the last experiment you ran?
<--- Score

231. What have been your experiences in defining long range Digital Forensics goals?
<--- Score

232. What trophy do you want on your mantle?
<--- Score

233. Who are four people whose careers you have enhanced?
<--- Score

234. Is Digital Forensics realistic, or are you setting yourself up for failure?
<--- Score

235. How do you cross-sell and up-sell your Digital Forensics success?
<--- Score

236. Why is Digital Forensics important for you now?
<--- Score

237. Which forensic tools and techniques are used?
<--- Score

238. Who is the main stakeholder, with ultimate responsibility for driving Digital Forensics forward?
<--- Score

239. What information should be included/ excluded?
<--- Score

240. Are you making progress, and are you making progress as Digital Forensics leaders?
<--- Score

241. What you are going to do to affect the numbers?
<--- Score

242. What are your personal philosophies regarding Digital Forensics and how do they influence your work?
<--- Score

243. Do you have the right capabilities and capacities?
<--- Score

244. If you do not follow, then how to lead?
<--- Score

245. Do you know what you are doing? And who do you call if you don't?
<--- Score

246. What are the essentials of internal Digital Forensics management?
<--- Score

247. Can you do all this work?
<--- Score

248. What is your formula for success in Digital Forensics ?
<--- Score

249. Any timeline missing in the evidence?
<--- Score

250. What kind of crime could a potential new hire have committed that would not only not disqualify him/her from being hired by your organization, but would actually indicate that he/she might be a particularly good fit?
<--- Score

251. How will you ensure you get what you expected?
<--- Score

252. Which forensic tools and techniques would most likely be used?
<--- Score

253. Are you maintaining a past–present–future perspective throughout the Digital Forensics discussion?
<--- Score

254. Who is on the team?
<--- Score

255. Who is responsible for Digital Forensics?
<--- Score

256. How much contingency will be available in the budget?

<--- Score

257. Do you think Digital Forensics accomplishes the goals you expect it to accomplish?

<--- Score

258. Do you have an implicit bias for capital investments over people investments?

<--- Score

259. What happens when a new employee joins the organization?

<--- Score

260. Do you see more potential in people than they do in themselves?

<--- Score

261. What communications with external parties might occur, if any?

<--- Score

262. What are the usability implications of Digital Forensics actions?

<--- Score

263. How would the use of forensic tools and techniques change if the worm disrupted network communications?

<--- Score

264. What are the top 3 things at the forefront of your Digital Forensics agendas for the next 3 years?

<--- Score

265. Where should be the place of enforcement?
<--- Score

266. Who, on the executive team or the board, has spoken to a customer recently?
<--- Score

267. What is being written to logs or disks?
<--- Score

268. What are the black box essential elements?
<--- Score

269. Biometrics Resources: What is Industry doing?
<--- Score

270. Who else should you help?
<--- Score

271. How do you stay inspired?
<--- Score

272. How do you engage the workforce, in addition to satisfying them?
<--- Score

273. Will there be any necessary staff changes (redundancies or new hires)?
<--- Score

274. Are the assumptions believable and achievable?
<--- Score

275. When information truly is ubiquitous, when reach and connectivity are completely global, when

computing resources are infinite, and when a whole new set of impossibilities are not only possible, but happening, what will that do to your business?
<--- Score

Add up total points for this section:
_____ = Total points for this section

Divided by: _____ (number of statements answered) = _____
Average score for this section

Transfer your score to the Digital Forensics Index at the beginning of the Self-Assessment.

Digital Forensics and Managing Projects, Criteria for Project Managers:

1.0 Initiating Process Group: Digital Forensics

1. Based on your Digital Forensics project communication management plan, what worked well?

2. Which six sigma dmaic phase focuses on why and how defects and errors occur?

3. What were things that you did very well and want to do the same again on the next Digital Forensics project?

4. If action is called for, what form should it take?

5. Were escalated issues resolved promptly?

6. Who is behind the Digital Forensics project?

7. Are there resources to maintain and support the outcome of the Digital Forensics project?

8. Do you understand the communication expectations for this Digital Forensics project?

9. Realistic - are the desired results expressed in a way that the team will be motivated and believe that the required level of involvement will be obtained?

10. Have the stakeholders identified all individual requirements pertaining to business process?

11. Do you understand the quality and control criteria that must be achieved for successful Digital Forensics

project completion?

12. How will you know you did it?

13. Will the Digital Forensics project meet the client requirements, and will it achieve the business success criteria that justified doing the Digital Forensics project in the first place?

14. If the risk event occurs, what will you do?

15. What will be the pressing issues of tomorrow?

16. What are the short and long term implications?

17. How well did the chosen processes produce the expected results?

18. The Digital Forensics project managers have maximum authority in which type of organization?

19. What areas does the group agree are the biggest success on the Digital Forensics project?

20. What do they need to know about the Digital Forensics project?

1.1 Project Charter: Digital Forensics

21. Where does all this information come from?

22. Name and describe the elements that deal with providing the detail?

23. Assumptions and constraints: what assumptions were made in defining the Digital Forensics project?

24. Why have you chosen the aim you have set forth?

25. For whom?

26. Strategic fit: what is the strategic initiative identifier for this Digital Forensics project?

27. Are there special technology requirements?

28. What does it need to do?

29. Where and how does the team fit within your organization structure?

30. Why is it important?

31. What changes can you make to improve?

32. What material?

33. Pop quiz – which are the same inputs as in the Digital Forensics project charter?

34. Is time of the essence?

35. Assumptions: what factors, for planning purposes, are you considering to be true?

36. How will you learn more about the process or system you are trying to improve?

37. Fit with other Products Compliments – Cannibalizes?

38. When?

39. Review the general mission What system will be affected by the improvement efforts?

40. Why do you need to manage scope?

1.2 Stakeholder Register: Digital Forensics

41. Who wants to talk about Security?

42. Is your organization ready for change?

43. Who are the stakeholders?

44. How much influence do they have on the Digital Forensics project?

45. What & Why?

46. What is the power of the stakeholder?

47. What opportunities exist to provide communications?

48. How should employers make voices heard?

49. How will reports be created?

50. What are the major Digital Forensics project milestones requiring communications or providing communications opportunities?

51. How big is the gap?

52. Who is managing stakeholder engagement?

1.3 Stakeholder Analysis Matrix: Digital Forensics

53. Timescales, deadlines and pressures?

54. Partnerships, agencies, distribution?

55. Sustainable financial backing?

56. Accreditations, qualifications, certifications?

57. Guiding question: what is the issue at stake?

58. Are you working on the right risks?

59. Does the stakeholder want to be involved or merely need to be informed about the Digital Forensics project and its process?

60. Could any of your organizations weaknesses seriously threaten development?

61. Arena: in what fields are the actors active, where are they present?

62. Usps (unique selling points)?

63. Who determines value?

64. Will the impacts be local, national or international?

65. Who is most interested in information about the topic and/or has previously initiated interest?

66. If the baseline is now, and if its improved it will be better than now?

67. Volumes, production, economies?

68. Participatory approach: how will key stakeholders participate in the Digital Forensics project?

69. Environmental effects?

70. Alliances: with which other actors is the actor allied, how are they interconnected?

71. How affected by the problem(s)?

2.0 Planning Process Group: Digital Forensics

72. To what extent is the program helping to influence your organizations policy framework?

73. Are work methodologies, financial instruments, etc. shared among departments, organizations and Digital Forensics projects?

74. To what extent do the intervention objectives and strategies of the Digital Forensics project respond to your organizations plans?

75. How can you tell when you are done?

76. In what way has the Digital Forensics project come up with innovative measures for problem-solving?

77. Explanation: is what the Digital Forensics project intents to solve a hard question?

78. How well will the chosen processes produce the expected results?

79. If you are late, will anybody notice?

80. Mitigate. what will you do to minimize the impact should a risk event occur?

81. Do the partners have sufficient financial capacity to keep up the benefits produced by the programme?

82. What should you do next?

83. In which Digital Forensics project management process group is the detailed Digital Forensics project budget created?

84. How well did the chosen processes fit the needs of the Digital Forensics project?

85. Is the pace of implementing the products of the program ensuring the completeness of the results of the Digital Forensics project?

86. You did your readings, yes?

87. Will you be replaced?

88. Did the program design/ implementation strategy adequately address the planning stage necessary to set up structures, hire staff etc.?

89. Have operating capacities been created and/or reinforced in partners?

90. Just how important is your work to the overall success of the Digital Forensics project?

2.1 Project Management Plan: Digital Forensics

91. What are the assigned resources?

92. Are there any client staffing expectations?

93. What if, for example, the positive direction and vision of your organization causes expected trends to change resulting in greater need than expected?

94. What worked well?

95. How do you organize the costs in the Digital Forensics project management plan?

96. What should you drop in order to add something new?

97. How can you best help your organization to develop consistent practices in Digital Forensics project management planning stages?

98. Are alternatives safe, functional, constructible, economical, reasonable and sustainable?

99. What happened during the process that you found interesting?

100. Does the selected plan protect privacy?

101. How do you manage time?

102. Who is the sponsor?

103. Is the engineering content at a feasibility level-of-detail, and is it sufficiently complete, to provide an adequate basis for the baseline cost estimate?

104. Do the proposed changes from the Digital Forensics project include any significant risks to safety?

105. Is there anything you would now do differently on your Digital Forensics project based on past experience?

106. Why do you manage integration?

107. Did the planning effort collaborate to develop solutions that integrate expertise, policies, programs, and Digital Forensics projects across entities?

108. Was the peer (technical) review of the cost estimates duly coordinated with the cost estimate center of expertise and addressed in the review documentation and certification?

109. Does the implementation plan have an appropriate division of responsibilities?

110. Are calculations and results of analyzes essentially correct?

2.2 Scope Management Plan: Digital Forensics

111. Are corrective actions taken when actual results are substantially different from detailed Digital Forensics project plan (variances)?

112. Staffing Requirements?

113. Do you have the reasons why the changes to your organizational systems and capabilities are required?

114. Where do scope processes fit in?

115. Has allowance been made for vacations, holidays, training (learning time for each team member), staff promotions & staff turnovers?

116. Are Digital Forensics project team members committed fulltime?

117. Have all necessary approvals been obtained?

118. What are the risks of not having good inter-organization cooperation on the Digital Forensics project?

119. Are the proposed Digital Forensics project purposes different than the previously authorized Digital Forensics project?

120. Materials available for performing the work?

121. Does the Digital Forensics project team have the skills necessary to successfully complete current Digital Forensics project(s) and support the application?

122. Have the procedures for identifying variances from estimates & adjusting the detailed work program been followed?

123. For which criterion is it tolerable not to meet the original parameters?

124. Were Digital Forensics project team members involved in the development of activity & task decomposition?

125. How much money have you spent?

126. Is an industry recognized mechanized support tool(s) being used for Digital Forensics project scheduling & tracking?

127. Has the selected plan been formulated using cost effectiveness and incremental analysis techniques?

128. Has a resource management plan been created?

129. Cost / benefit analysis?

2.3 Requirements Management Plan: Digital Forensics

130. Who has the authority to reject Digital Forensics project requirements?

131. Do you understand the role that each stakeholder will play in the requirements process?

132. Why manage requirements?

133. When and how will a requirements baseline be established in this Digital Forensics project?

134. How will requirements be managed?

135. After the requirements are gathered and set forth on the requirements register, theyre little more than a laundry list of items. Some may be duplicates, some might conflict with others and some will be too broad or too vague to understand. Describe how the requirements will be analyzed. Who will perform the analysis?

136. What went wrong?

137. Did you use declarative statements?

138. How will the information be distributed?

139. Is there formal agreement on who has authority to request a change in requirements?

140. What is the earliest finish date for this Digital Forensics project if it is scheduled to start on ...?

141. Will you have access to stakeholders when you need them?

142. How will you communicate scheduled tasks to other team members?

143. How do you know that you have done this right?

144. Is the system software (non-operating system) new to the IT Digital Forensics project team?

145. Did you get proper approvals?

146. Will the Digital Forensics project requirements become approved in writing?

147. What performance metrics will be used?

148. Is it new or replacing an existing business system or process?

149. Did you distinguish the scope of work the contractor(s) will be required to do?

2.4 Requirements Documentation: Digital Forensics

150. Where do system and software requirements come from, what are sources?

151. If applicable; are there issues linked with the fact that this is an offshore Digital Forensics project?

152. Where are business rules being captured?

153. Is new technology needed?

154. What is a show stopper in the requirements?

155. Have the benefits identified with the system being identified clearly?

156. Are all functions required by the customer included?

157. Do technical resources exist?

158. Are there legal issues?

159. Can the requirements be checked?

160. Who provides requirements?

161. How does what is being described meet the business need?

162. Does your organization restrict technical

alternatives?

163. What marketing channels do you want to use: e-mail, letter or sms?

164. How to document system requirements?

165. How does the proposed Digital Forensics project contribute to the overall objectives of your organization?

166. Validity. does the system provide the functions which best support the customers needs?

167. How much does requirements engineering cost?

168. Completeness. are all functions required by the customer included?

169. Has requirements gathering uncovered information that would necessitate changes?

2.5 Requirements Traceability Matrix: Digital Forensics

170. How will it affect the stakeholders personally in their career?

171. Is there a requirements traceability process in place?

172. How do you manage scope?

173. What percentage of Digital Forensics projects are producing traceability matrices between requirements and other work products?

174. Why do you manage scope?

175. Do you have a clear understanding of all subcontracts in place?

176. Why use a WBS?

177. What are the chronologies, contingencies, consequences, criteria?

178. Will you use a Requirements Traceability Matrix?

179. What is the WBS?

180. How small is small enough?

181. Describe the process for approving requirements so they can be added to the traceability matrix and

Digital Forensics project work can be performed. Will the Digital Forensics project requirements become approved in writing?

2.6 Project Scope Statement: Digital Forensics

182. Is the change control process documented and on file?

183. What is a process you might recommend to verify the accuracy of the research deliverable?

184. Is an issue management process documented and filed?

185. Is there an information system for the Digital Forensics project?

186. Elements that deal with providing the detail?

187. Will the Digital Forensics project risks be managed according to the Digital Forensics projects risk management process?

188. Once its defined, what is the stability of the Digital Forensics project scope?

189. Was planning completed before the Digital Forensics project was initiated?

190. Are the meetings set up to have assigned note takers that will add action/issues to the issue list?

191. Are there specific processes you will use to evaluate and approve/reject changes?

192. How will you haverify the accuracy of the work of the Digital Forensics project, and what constitutes acceptance of the deliverables?

193. Will the qa related information be reported regularly as part of the status reporting mechanisms?

194. Are there backup strategies for key members of the Digital Forensics project?

195. Will the risk plan be updated on a regular and frequent basis?

196. Are there adequate Digital Forensics project control systems?

197. Elements of scope management that deal with concept development ?

2.7 Assumption and Constraint Log: Digital Forensics

198. Diagrams and tables are included to account for complex concepts and increase overall readability?

199. If it is out of compliance, should the process be amended or should the Plan be amended?

200. What if failure during recovery?

201. Do documented requirements exist for all critical components and areas, including technical, business, interfaces, performance, security and conversion requirements?

202. Does the document/deliverable meet general requirements (for example, statement of work) for all deliverables?

203. Model-building: what data-analytic strategies are useful when building proportional-hazards models?

204. Is this process still needed?

205. Is the process working, and people are not executing in compliance of the process?

206. What do you log?

207. Does a specific action and/or state that is known to violate security policy occur?

208. Were the system requirements formally reviewed prior to initiating the design phase?

209. How many Digital Forensics project staff does this specific process affect?

210. Do the requirements meet the standards of correctness, completeness, consistency, accuracy, and readability?

211. How are new requirements or changes to requirements identified?

212. Does the plan conform to standards?

213. Are there procedures in place to effectively manage interdependencies with other Digital Forensics projects / systems?

214. Is staff trained on the software technologies that are being used on the Digital Forensics project?

215. Is the current scope of the Digital Forensics project substantially different than that originally defined in the approved Digital Forensics project plan?

216. Have Digital Forensics project management standards and procedures been established and documented?

217. Are requirements management tracking tools and procedures in place?

2.8 Work Breakdown Structure: Digital Forensics

218. Is it a change in scope?

219. Do you need another level?

220. What is the probability of completing the Digital Forensics project in less that xx days?

221. When does it have to be done?

222. Is it still viable?

223. When would you develop a Work Breakdown Structure?

224. How big is a work-package?

225. What has to be done?

226. Why would you develop a Work Breakdown Structure?

227. Who has to do it?

228. When do you stop?

229. Is the work breakdown structure (wbs) defined and is the scope of the Digital Forensics project clear with assigned deliverable owners?

230. Where does it take place?

231. How far down?

232. What is the probability that the Digital Forensics project duration will exceed xx weeks?

233. How will you and your Digital Forensics project team define the Digital Forensics projects scope and work breakdown structure?

234. Why is it useful?

235. How many levels?

236. Can you make it?

237. How much detail?

2.9 WBS Dictionary: Digital Forensics

238. Do work packages reflect the actual way in which the work will be done and are they meaningful products or management-oriented subdivisions of a higher level element of work?

239. What is the goal?

240. Time-phased control account budgets?

241. Identify potential or actual overruns and underruns?

242. Are detailed work packages planned as far in advance as practicable?

243. Does the contractor require sufficient detailed planning of control accounts to constrain the application of budget initially allocated for future effort to current effort?

244. Intermediate schedules, as required, which provide a logical sequence from the master schedule to the control account level?

245. Are overhead budgets and costs being handled according to the disclosure statement when applicable, or otherwise properly classified (for example, engineering overhead, IR&D)?

246. Are estimates of costs at completion generated in a rational, consistent manner?

247. Are overhead costs budgets established on a basis consistent with anticipated direct business base?

248. Are the rates for allocating costs from each indirect cost pool to contracts updated as necessary to ensure a realistic monthly allocation of indirect costs without significant year-end adjustments?

249. Does the contractor use objective results, design reviews and tests to trace schedule performance?

250. Is the entire contract planned in time-phased control accounts to the extent practicable?

251. Contractor financial periods; for example, annual?

252. Performance to date and material commitment?

253. Evaluate the performance of operating organizations?

254. What are you counting on?

255. Wbs elements contractually specified for reporting of status to you (lowest level only)?

2.10 Schedule Management Plan: Digital Forensics

256. What strengths do you have?

257. Is there an issues management plan in place?

258. Has the business need been clearly defined?

259. Are issues raised, assessed, actioned, and resolved in a timely and efficient manner?

260. Were the budget estimates reasonable?

261. Are changes in scope (deliverable commitments) agreed to by all affected groups & individuals?

262. Is there a formal process for updating the Digital Forensics project baseline?

263. Are the appropriate IT resources adequate to meet planned commitments?

264. Has the Digital Forensics project scope been baselined?

265. Is pert / critical path or equivalent methodology being used?

266. Have the key functions and capabilities been defined and assigned to each release or iteration?

267. Has your organization readiness assessment

been conducted?

268. Are Digital Forensics project team members involved in detailed estimating and scheduling?

269. How relevant is this attribute to this Digital Forensics project or audit?

270. Do all stakeholders know how to access this repository and where to find the Digital Forensics project documentation?

271. Are all attributes of the activities defined, including risk and uncertainty?

272. Are the Digital Forensics project plans updated on a frequent basis?

273. Are staff skills known and available for each task?

274. Do Digital Forensics project managers participating in the Digital Forensics project know the Digital Forensics projects true status first hand?

275. Is the ims used by all levels of management for Digital Forensics project implementation and control?

2.11 Activity List: Digital Forensics

276. In what sequence?

277. How detailed should a Digital Forensics project get?

278. For other activities, how much delay can be tolerated?

279. What are the critical bottleneck activities?

280. Who will perform the work?

281. How difficult will it be to do specific activities on this Digital Forensics project?

282. What went right?

283. Where will it be performed?

284. What is the LF and LS for each activity?

285. Is there anything planned that does not need to be here?

286. How can the Digital Forensics project be displayed graphically to better visualize the activities?

287. How much slack is available in the Digital Forensics project?

288. Should you include sub-activities?

289. Can you determine the activity that must finish, before this activity can start?

290. The wbs is developed as part of a joint planning session. and how do you know that youhave done this right?

291. Are the required resources available or need to be acquired?

292. What is the total time required to complete the Digital Forensics project if no delays occur?

293. What is your organizations history in doing similar activities?

2.12 Activity Attributes: Digital Forensics

294. Resources to accomplish the work?

295. Can you re-assign any activities to another resource to resolve an over-allocation?

296. Were there other ways you could have organized the data to achieve similar results?

297. Where else does it apply?

298. What is missing?

299. Activity: fair or not fair?

300. How difficult will it be to complete specific activities on this Digital Forensics project?

301. Activity: what is In the Bag?

302. Have you identified the Activity Leveling Priority code value on each activity?

303. How many resources do you need to complete the work scope within a limit of X number of days?

304. Does your organization of the data change its meaning?

305. How difficult will it be to do specific activities on this Digital Forensics project?

306. Activity: what is Missing?

307. Time for overtime?

308. Have constraints been applied to the start and finish milestones for the phases?

309. Do you feel very comfortable with your prediction?

310. Are the required resources available?

2.13 Milestone List: Digital Forensics

311. How late can the activity finish?

312. Reliability of data, plan predictability?

313. How late can the activity start?

314. When will the Digital Forensics project be complete?

315. Vital contracts and partners?

316. How will you get the word out to customers?

317. Obstacles faced?

318. Legislative effects?

319. Political effects?

320. Continuity, supply chain robustness?

321. Own known vulnerabilities?

322. Which path is the critical path?

323. What background experience, skills, and strengths does the team bring to your organization?

324. Marketing - reach, distribution, awareness?

325. How soon can the activity finish?

326. Gaps in capabilities?

327. What specific improvements did you make to the Digital Forensics project proposal since the previous time?

2.14 Network Diagram: Digital Forensics

328. What job or jobs could run concurrently?

329. If the Digital Forensics project network diagram cannot change and you have extra personnel resources, what is the BEST thing to do?

330. What controls the start and finish of a job?

331. Which type of network diagram allows you to depict four types of dependencies?

332. What is the probability of completing the Digital Forensics project in less that xx days?

333. Planning: who, how long, what to do?

334. If a current contract exists, can you provide the vendor name, contract start, and contract expiration date?

335. What must be completed before an activity can be started?

336. What activities must occur simultaneously with this activity?

337. Are you on time?

338. What can be done concurrently?

339. What to do and When?

340. What are the Key Success Factors?

341. Where do schedules come from?

342. What job or jobs follow it?

343. Exercise: what is the probability that the Digital Forensics project duration will exceed xx weeks?

344. What job or jobs precede it?

345. Where do you schedule uncertainty time?

346. What activity must be completed immediately before this activity can start?

2.15 Activity Resource Requirements: Digital Forensics

347. Organizational Applicability?

348. How many signatures do you require on a check and does this match what is in your policy and procedures?

349. What are constraints that you might find during the Human Resource Planning process?

350. Anything else?

351. Why do you do that?

352. Do you use tools like decomposition and rolling-wave planning to produce the activity list and other outputs?

353. Are there unresolved issues that need to be addressed?

354. When does monitoring begin?

355. Other support in specific areas?

356. Which logical relationship does the PDM use most often?

357. What is the Work Plan Standard?

358. How do you handle petty cash?

2.16 Resource Breakdown Structure: Digital Forensics

359. What is each stakeholders desired outcome for the Digital Forensics project?

360. What is the purpose of assigning and documenting responsibility?

361. Who delivers the information?

362. Which resource planning tool provides information on resource responsibility and accountability?

363. What defines a successful Digital Forensics project?

364. How should the information be delivered?

365. When do they need the information?

366. What is the difference between % Complete and % work?

367. What can you do to improve productivity?

368. Why time management?

369. How can this help you with team building?

370. How difficult will it be to do specific activities on this Digital Forensics project?

371. What is the number one predictor of a groups productivity?

372. Goals for the Digital Forensics project. What is each stakeholders desired outcome for the Digital Forensics project?

373. Who will be used as a Digital Forensics project team member?

374. What is the primary purpose of the human resource plan?

2.17 Activity Duration Estimates: Digital Forensics

375. What is involved in the solicitation process?

376. Are team building activities completed to improve team performance?

377. Sigma Digital Forensics project?

378. Are contractor costs, schedule and technical performance monitored throughout the Digital Forensics project?

379. Are operational definitions created to identify quality measurement criteria for specific activities?

380. List five reasons why organizations outsource. Why is there a growing trend in outsourcing, especially in the government?

381. How many different communications channels does a Digital Forensics project team with six people have?

382. What are the main processes included in Digital Forensics project quality management?

383. Is the cost performance monitored to identify variances from the plan?

384. Is training acquired to enhance the skills, knowledge and capabilities of the Digital Forensics

project team?

385. Are procedures documented for managing risks?

386. Are activity dependencies documented?

387. What functions does this software provide that cannot be done easily using other tools such as a spreadsheet or database?

388. If Digital Forensics project time and cost are not as important as the number of resources used each month, which is the BEST thing to do?

389. Do Digital Forensics project team members work in the same physical location to enhance team performance?

390. Is the Digital Forensics project performing better or worse than planned?

391. Calculate the expected duration for an activity that has a most likely time of 5, a pessimistic time of 13, and a optimiztic time of 3?

392. Can they use the already stated?

393. Are training needs identified when resources do not have the required skills to complete Digital Forensics project activities?

394. Are inspections completed to determine if the results comply with the requirements?

2.18 Duration Estimating Worksheet: Digital Forensics

395. Value pocket identification & quantification what are value pockets?

396. When does your organization expect to be able to complete it?

397. Is the Digital Forensics project responsive to community need?

398. Why estimate costs?

399. What questions do you have?

400. Is a construction detail attached (to aid in explanation)?

401. Will the Digital Forensics project collaborate with the local community and leverage resources?

402. Is this operation cost effective?

403. What is an Average Digital Forensics project?

404. What is next?

405. Does the Digital Forensics project provide innovative ways for stakeholders to overcome obstacles or deliver better outcomes?

406. Define the work as completely as possible. What

work will be included in the Digital Forensics project?

407. Small or large Digital Forensics project?

408. Can the Digital Forensics project be constructed as planned?

409. How should ongoing costs be monitored to try to keep the Digital Forensics project within budget?

410. What is cost and Digital Forensics project cost management?

411. What is the total time required to complete the Digital Forensics project if no delays occur?

412. What info is needed?

2.19 Project Schedule: Digital Forensics

413. Eliminate unnecessary activities. Are there activities that came from a template or previous Digital Forensics project that are not applicable on this phase of this Digital Forensics project?

414. Is the Digital Forensics project schedule available for all Digital Forensics project team members to review?

415. Is the structure for tracking the Digital Forensics project schedule well defined and assigned to a specific individual?

416. If there are any qualifying green components to this Digital Forensics project, what portion of the total Digital Forensics project cost is green?

417. Your best shot for providing estimations how complex/how much work does the activity require?

418. Digital Forensics project work estimates Who is managing the work estimate quality of work tasks in the Digital Forensics project schedule?

419. What is the difference?

420. How closely did the initial Digital Forensics project Schedule compare with the actual schedule?

421. How can you minimize or control changes to

Digital Forensics project schedules?

422. Should you have a test for each code module?

423. Is there a Schedule Management Plan that establishes the criteria and activities for developing, monitoring and controlling the Digital Forensics project schedule?

424. Does the condition or event threaten the Digital Forensics projects objectives in any ways?

425. What is the purpose of a Digital Forensics project schedule?

426. What is the most mis-scheduled part of process?

427. How do you use schedules?

428. Why is software Digital Forensics project disaster so common?

429. How can you shorten the schedule?

2.20 Cost Management Plan: Digital Forensics

430. Have Digital Forensics project team accountabilities & responsibilities been clearly defined?

431. Are adequate resources provided for the quality assurance function?

432. If you sold 10x widgets on a day, what would the affect on costs be?

433. Is current scope of the Digital Forensics project substantially different than that originally defined?

434. What is Digital Forensics project management?

435. The definition of the Digital Forensics project scope what needs to be accomplished?

436. Is it a Digital Forensics project?

437. Contractors scope – how will contractors scope be defined when contracts are let?

438. Has the Digital Forensics project manager been identified?

439. Vac -variance at completion, how much over/ under budget do you expect to be?

440. Does the schedule include Digital Forensics

project management time and change request analysis time?

441. Are risk triggers captured?

442. Has a structured approach been used to break work effort into manageable components (WBS)?

443. Have external dependencies been captured in the schedule?

444. Have adequate resources been provided by management to ensure Digital Forensics project success?

445. What is an Acceptance Management Process?

446. Have all documents been archived in a Digital Forensics project repository for each release?

447. Are status reports received per the Digital Forensics project Plan?

448. Are the people assigned to the Digital Forensics project sufficiently qualified?

2.21 Activity Cost Estimates: Digital Forensics

449. How do you treat administrative costs in the activity inventory?

450. What makes a good expected result statement?

451. Certification of actual expenditures?

452. What is Digital Forensics project cost management?

453. One way to define activities is to consider how organization employees describe jobs to families and friends. You basically want to know, What do you do?

454. Who determines the quality and expertise of contractors?

455. What areas were overlooked on this Digital Forensics project?

456. What is the Digital Forensics projects sustainability strategy that will ensure Digital Forensics project results will endure or be sustained?

457. Why do you manage cost?

458. Were the tasks or work products prepared by the consultant useful?

459. What is the last item a Digital Forensics project

manager must do to finalize Digital Forensics project close-out?

460. Where can you get activity reports?

461. Will you need to provide essential services information about activities?

462. What cost data should be used to estimate costs during the 2-year follow-up period?

463. How and when do you enter into Digital Forensics project Procurement Management?

464. If you are asked to lower your estimate because the price is too high, what are your options?

465. How do you change activities?

466. Who & what determines the need for contracted services?

2.22 Cost Estimating Worksheet: Digital Forensics

467. Can a trend be established from historical performance data on the selected measure and are the criteria for using trend analysis or forecasting methods met?

468. Identify the timeframe necessary to monitor progress and collect data to determine how the selected measure has changed?

469. Does the Digital Forensics project provide innovative ways for stakeholders to overcome obstacles or deliver better outcomes?

470. What additional Digital Forensics project(s) could be initiated as a result of this Digital Forensics project?

471. Will the Digital Forensics project collaborate with the local community and leverage resources?

472. What is the estimated labor cost today based upon this information?

473. Is it feasible to establish a control group arrangement?

474. What will others want?

475. Ask: are others positioned to know, are others credible, and will others cooperate?

476. Is the Digital Forensics project responsive to community need?

477. How will the results be shared and to whom?

478. What costs are to be estimated?

479. Who is best positioned to know and assist in identifying corresponding factors?

480. What can be included?

481. What is the purpose of estimating?

482. What happens to any remaining funds not used?

2.23 Cost Baseline: Digital Forensics

483. Has the documentation relating to operation and maintenance of the product(s) or service(s) been delivered to, and accepted by, operations management?

484. How likely is it to go wrong?

485. Are you asking management for something as a result of this update?

486. Has the Digital Forensics projected annual cost to operate and maintain the product(s) or service(s) been approved and funded?

487. Have all approved changes to the schedule baseline been identified and impact on the Digital Forensics project documented?

488. When should cost estimates be developed?

489. Has the actual cost of the Digital Forensics project (or Digital Forensics project phase) been tallied and compared to the approved budget?

490. Digital Forensics project goals -should others be reconsidered?

491. What is the reality?

492. Has the Digital Forensics project (or Digital Forensics project phase) been evaluated against each objective established in the product description and

Integrated Digital Forensics project Plan?

493. Have all approved changes to the Digital Forensics project requirement been identified and impact on the performance, cost, and schedule baselines documented?

494. What do you want to measure ?

495. What weaknesses do you have?

496. Have all the product or service deliverables been accepted by the customer?

497. Has operations management formally accepted responsibility for operating and maintaining the product(s) or service(s) delivered by the Digital Forensics project?

498. What is the consequence?

499. What threats might prevent you from getting there?

500. How difficult will it be to do specific tasks on the Digital Forensics project?

2.24 Quality Management Plan: Digital Forensics

501. Does the Digital Forensics project have a formal Digital Forensics project Plan?

502. Why quality management?

503. How do you ensure that your sampling methods and procedures meet your data quality objectives?

504. Who is responsible for writing the qapp?

505. How does your organization address regulatory, legal, and ethical compliance?

506. Have you eliminated all duplicative tasks or manual efforts, where appropriate?

507. With the five whys method, the team considers why the issue being explored occurred. do others then take that initial answer and ask why?

508. What procedures are used to determine if you use, and the number of split, replicate or duplicate samples taken at a site?

509. How are senior leaders, employees, and your organization involved in supporting the community?

510. When reporting to different audiences, do you vary the form or type of report?

511. Written by multiple authors and in multiple writing styles?

512. Have Digital Forensics project management standards and procedures been established and documented?

513. Do you keep back-up copies of any data?

514. Does the program conduct field testing?

515. What other teams / processes would be impacted by changes to the current process, and how?

516. What is positive about the current process?

517. What methods are used?

2.25 Quality Metrics: Digital Forensics

518. Do the operators focus on determining; is there anything you need to worry about?

519. Should a modifier be included?

520. What method of measurement do you use?

521. How does one achieve stability?

522. Did evaluation start on time?

523. When is the security analysis testing complete?

524. Are quality metrics defined?

525. How should customers provide input?

526. Were quality attributes reported?

527. Are there any open risk issues?

528. Are documents on hand to provide explanations of privacy and confidentiality?

529. Were number of defects identified?

530. Does risk analysis documentation meet standards?

531. Do you know how much profit a 10% decrease in waste would generate?

532. Which data do others need in one place to target areas of improvement?

533. Is quality culture a competitive advantage?

534. There are many reasons to shore up quality-related metrics, and what metrics are important?

535. What metrics are important and most beneficial to measure?

536. Was review conducted per standard protocols?

537. Has it met internal or external standards?

2.26 Process Improvement Plan: Digital Forensics

538. If a process improvement framework is being used, which elements will help the problems and goals listed?

539. What personnel are the sponsors for that initiative?

540. What makes people good SPI coaches?

541. The motive is determined by asking, Why do you want to achieve this goal?

542. Why do you want to achieve the goal?

543. Management commitment at all levels?

544. Are you making progress on the goals?

545. Does your process ensure quality?

546. Are you meeting the quality standards?

547. What is quality and how will you ensure it?

548. Modeling current processes is great, and will you ever see a return on that investment?

549. What personnel are the change agents for your initiative?

550. Purpose of goal: the motive is determined by asking, why do you want to achieve this goal?

551. Are you following the quality standards?

552. Are you making progress on the improvement framework?

553. Has a process guide to collect the data been developed?

554. What personnel are the coaches for your initiative?

555. Where do you want to be?

556. What personnel are the champions for the initiative?

557. Everyone agrees on what process improvement is, right?

2.27 Responsibility Assignment Matrix: Digital Forensics

558. Are authorized changes being incorporated in a timely manner?

559. Undistributed budgets, if any?

560. Who is going to do that work?

561. Is the anticipated (firm and potential) business base Digital Forensics projected in a rational, consistent manner?

562. When performing is split among two or more roles, is the work clearly defined so that the efforts are coordinated and the communication is clear?

563. Does the contractor use objective results, design reviews, and tests to trace schedule?

564. Are control accounts opened and closed based on the start and completion of work contained therein?

565. Are records maintained to show how management reserves are used?

566. How do you assist them to be as productive as possible?

567. Do you need to convince people that its well worth the time and effort?

568. Not any rs, as, or cs: if an identified role is only informed, should others be eliminated from the matrix?

569. Does each role with Accountable responsibility have the authority within your organization to make the required decisions?

570. What tool can show you individual and group allocations?

571. Are people encouraged to bring up issues?

572. Does the Digital Forensics project need to be analyzed further to uncover additional responsibilities?

573. The staff characteristics – is the group or the person capable to work together as a team?

574. Does the contractors system include procedures for measuring the performance of critical subcontractors?

2.28 Roles and Responsibilities: Digital Forensics

575. Implementation of actions: Who are the responsible units?

576. Are your policies supportive of a culture of quality data?

577. Accountabilities: what are the roles and responsibilities of individual team members?

578. Are governance roles and responsibilities documented?

579. How well did the Digital Forensics project Team understand the expectations of specific roles and responsibilities?

580. What should you do now to ensure that you are meeting all expectations of your current position?

581. Do the values and practices inherent in the culture of your organization foster or hinder the process?

582. How is your work-life balance?

583. Where are you most strong as a supervisor?

584. Key conclusions and recommendations: Are conclusions and recommendations relevant and acceptable?

585. Is the data complete?

586. What expectations were met?

587. Attainable / achievable: the goal is attainable; can you actually accomplish the goal?

588. What areas of supervision are challenging for you?

589. What should you do now to prepare for your career 5+ years from now?

590. Authority: what areas/Digital Forensics projects in your work do you have the authority to decide upon and act on the already stated decisions?

591. What specific behaviors did you observe?

592. Once the responsibilities are defined for the Digital Forensics project, have the deliverables, roles and responsibilities been clearly communicated to every participant?

593. Be specific; avoid generalities. Thank you and great work alone are insufficient. What exactly do you appreciate and why?

2.29 Human Resource Management Plan: Digital Forensics

594. What did you have to assume to be true to complete the charter?

595. Who is evaluated?

596. Do Digital Forensics project teams & team members report on status / activities / progress?

597. Is the Digital Forensics project sponsor clearly communicating the business case or rationale for why this Digital Forensics project is needed?

598. Are schedule deliverables actually delivered?

599. Is there an onboarding process in place?

600. Is the Digital Forensics project schedule available for all Digital Forensics project team members to review?

601. Are updated Digital Forensics project time & resource estimates reasonable based on the current Digital Forensics project stage?

602. Does the resource management plan include a personnel development plan?

603. Are tasks tracked by hours?

604. Are software metrics formally captured, analyzed

and used as a basis for other Digital Forensics project estimates?

605. Are the right people being attracted and retained to meet the future challenges?

606. Are the Digital Forensics project team members located locally to the users/stakeholders?

607. Are milestone deliverables effectively tracked and compared to Digital Forensics project plan?

608. Is the assigned Digital Forensics project manager a PMP (Certified Digital Forensics project manager) and experienced?

2.30 Communications Management Plan: Digital Forensics

609. Are there too many who have an interest in some aspect of your work?

610. What to know?

611. What steps can you take for a positive relationship?

612. Who is the stakeholder?

613. Are there potential barriers between the team and the stakeholder?

614. Do you prepare stakeholder engagement plans?

615. Where do team members get information?

616. How did the term stakeholder originate?

617. What data is going to be required?

618. What help do you and your team need from the stakeholder?

619. What are the interrelationships?

620. How were corresponding initiatives successful?

621. Are there common objectives between the team and the stakeholder?

622. Why do you manage communications?

623. Why manage stakeholders?

624. How much time does it take to do it?

625. What approaches to you feel are the best ones to use?

626. Will messages be directly related to the release strategy or phases of the Digital Forensics project?

627. What communications method?

628. Who to share with?

2.31 Risk Management Plan: Digital Forensics

629. What are the chances the risk event will occur?

630. Was an original risk assessment/risk management plan completed?

631. What other risks are created by choosing an avoidance strategy?

632. Internal technical and management reviews?

633. How quickly does this item need to be resolved?

634. How much risk can you tolerate?

635. What is the cost to the Digital Forensics project if it does occur?

636. Are status updates being made on schedule and are the updates clearly described?

637. Can you stabilize dynamic risk factors?

638. How will the Digital Forensics project know if your organizations risk response actions were effective?

639. Which risks should get the attention?

640. Are the software tools integrated with each other?

641. Degree of confidence in estimated size estimate?

642. Do end-users have realistic expectations?

643. Is Digital Forensics project scope stable?

644. How is risk identification performed?

645. Does the Digital Forensics project team have experience with the technology to be implemented?

646. Do you have a consistent repeatable process that is actually used?

647. Should the risk be taken at all?

648. Are people attending meetings and doing work?

2.32 Risk Register: Digital Forensics

649. What action, if any, has been taken to respond to the risk?

650. What can be done about it?

651. Risk probability and impact: how will the probabilities and impacts of risk items be assessed?

652. Preventative actions - planned actions to reduce the likelihood a risk will occur and/or reduce the seriousness should it occur. What should you do now?

653. Are your objectives at risk?

654. Methodology: how will risk management be performed on this Digital Forensics project?

655. How are risks identified?

656. User involvement: do you have the right users?

657. What is your current and future risk profile?

658. Assume the risk event or situation happens, what would the impact be?

659. Financial risk -can your organization afford to undertake the Digital Forensics project?

660. How is a Community Risk Register created?

661. What are you going to do to limit the Digital

Forensics projects risk exposure due to the identified risks?

662. What further options might be available for responding to the risk?

663. People risk -are people with appropriate skills available to help complete the Digital Forensics project?

664. Are implemented controls working as others should?

665. Can the likelihood and impact of failing to achieve corresponding recommendations and action plans be assessed?

666. Do you require further engagement?

667. Amongst the action plans and recommendations that you have to introduce are there some that could stop or delay the overall program?

668. What are the major risks facing the Digital Forensics project?

2.33 Probability and Impact Assessment: Digital Forensics

669. Does the customer have a solid idea of what is required?

670. What will be cost of redeployment of personnel?

671. Has something like this been done before?

672. Can it be enlarged by drawing people from other areas of your organization?

673. Are flexibility and reuse paramount?

674. Are Digital Forensics project requirements stable?

675. What are the current demands of the customer?

676. What is the likely future demand of the customer?

677. Are the risk data complete?

678. How much risk do others need to take?

679. Which risks need to move on to Perform Quantitative Risk Analysis?

680. What is the likelihood of a breakthrough?

681. Which of your Digital Forensics projects should be selected when compared with other Digital

Forensics projects?

682. What should be the requirement of organizational restructuring as each subDigital Forensics project goes through a different lifecycle phase?

683. Would avoiding any of corresponding impact the Digital Forensics projects chance of success?

684. What are the current requirements of the customer?

685. Have decisions that should be left open because of inadequate information on technology been identified and responsibility assigned for reducing the uncertainty?

686. My Digital Forensics project leader has suddenly left your organization, what do you do?

687. Why has this particular mode of contracting been chosen?

2.34 Probability and Impact Matrix: Digital Forensics

688. Costs associated with late delivery or a defective product?

689. What should be done NEXT?

690. If you can not fix it, how do you do it differently?

691. Which of your Digital Forensics projects should be selected when compared with other Digital Forensics projects?

692. How solid are the price-volume Digital Forensics projections?

693. What new technologies are being explored in the same area?

694. What are ways to measure and evaluate risks?

695. How do you manage Digital Forensics project Risk?

696. Who has experience with this?

697. What are the probable external agencies to act as Digital Forensics project manager?

698. Do you have specific methods that you use for each phase of the process?

699. Have you worked with the customer in the past?

700. Mandated specific features?

701. How realistic is the timing of introduction?

702. Will there be an increase in the political conservatism?

703. What is the level of commitment and professionalism?

704. How would you suggest monitoring for risk transition indicators?

705. Is the delay in one subDigital Forensics project going to affect another?

706. What risks are necessary to achieve success?

2.35 Risk Data Sheet: Digital Forensics

707. How can hazards be reduced?

708. Do effective diagnostic tests exist?

709. What is the environment within which you operate (social trends, economic, community values, broad based participation, national directions etc.)?

710. Has a sensitivity analysis been carried out?

711. What is the chance that it will happen?

712. Will revised controls lead to tolerable risk levels?

713. Are new hazards created?

714. Has the most cost-effective solution been chosen?

715. Is the data sufficiently specified in terms of the type of failure being analyzed, and its frequency or probability?

716. What were the Causes that contributed?

717. What will be the consequences if it happens?

718. Type of risk identified?

719. What are you trying to achieve (Objectives)?

720. What do people affected think about the need

for, and practicality of preventive measures?

721. What are the main threats to your existence?

722. How do you handle product safely?

723. What can you do?

724. Whom do you serve (customers)?

725. What actions can be taken to eliminate or remove risk?

726. What if client refuses?

2.36 Procurement Management Plan: Digital Forensics

727. Have lessons learned been conducted after each Digital Forensics project release?

728. Is the structure for tracking the Digital Forensics project schedule well defined and assigned to a specific individual?

729. Are vendor invoices audited for accuracy before payment?

730. Does the detailed work plan match the complexity of tasks with the capabilities of personnel?

731. Similar Digital Forensics projects?

732. Are trade-offs between accepting the risk and mitigating the risk identified?

733. Are updated Digital Forensics project time & resource estimates reasonable based on the current Digital Forensics project stage?

734. How will multiple providers be managed?

735. Are the payment terms being followed?

736. Are Digital Forensics project team members involved in detailed estimating and scheduling?

737. Is there an on-going process in place to monitor

Digital Forensics project risks?

738. Are metrics used to evaluate and manage Vendors?

739. Has a Digital Forensics project Communications Plan been developed?

740. Has a sponsor been identified?

741. Is the current scope of the Digital Forensics project substantially different than that originally defined?

742. Is a stakeholder management plan in place that covers topics?

743. Has Digital Forensics project success criteria been defined?

2.37 Source Selection Criteria: Digital Forensics

744. What are the limitations on pre-competitive range communications?

745. What is the effect of the debriefing schedule on potential protests?

746. Has all proposal data been loaded?

747. What instructions should be provided regarding oral presentations?

748. Which contract type places the most risk on the seller?

749. What should be considered?

750. What information may not be provided?

751. How should oral presentations be evaluated?

752. Comparison of each offers prices to the estimated prices -are there significant differences?

753. What can not be disclosed?

754. What risks were identified in the proposals?

755. In the technical/management area, what criteria do you use to determine the final evaluation ratings?

756. Have team members been adequately trained?

757. What are the guidelines regarding award without considerations?

758. How can solicitation Schedules be improved to yield more effective price competition?

759. Do you have a plan to document consensus results including disposition of any disagreement by individual evaluators?

760. Do you have designated specific forms or worksheets?

761. In order of importance, which evaluation criteria are the most critical to the determination of your overall rating?

762. Who is on the Source Selection Advisory Committee?

763. How should the solicitation aspects regarding past performance be structured?

2.38 Stakeholder Management Plan: Digital Forensics

764. Where will verification occur, and by whom?

765. What potential impact does the stakeholder have on the Digital Forensics project?

766. What are the criteria for selecting suppliers of off the shelf products?

767. Are there processes in place to ensure internal consistency between the source code components?

768. Who will perform the review(s)?

769. What preventative action can be taken to reduce the likelihood a risk will be realised?

770. Is there a Steering Committee in place?

771. Are vendor contract reports, reviews and visits conducted periodically?

772. Are procurement deliverables arriving on time and to specification?

773. Is the quality assurance team identified?

774. Were Digital Forensics project team members involved in detailed estimating and scheduling?

775. Is stakeholder involvement adequate?

776. Who would sign off on the charter?

777. What guidelines or procedures currently exist that must be adhered to (eg departmental accounting procedures)?

778. What is the primary function of the Activity Decomposition Decision Tree?

779. What potential impact does the Digital Forensics project have on the stakeholder?

780. Have stakeholder accountabilities & responsibilities been clearly defined?

781. Is the process working, and are people executing in compliance of the process?

2.39 Change Management Plan: Digital Forensics

782. What tasks are needed?

783. Does this change represent a completely new process for your organization, or a different application of an existing process?

784. What are the specific target groups/audiences that will be impacted by this change?

785. When developing your communication plan do you address : When should the given message be communicated?

786. Do there need to be new channels developed?

787. When to start change management?

788. Identify the current level of skills and knowledge and behaviours of the group that will be impacted on. What prerequisite knowledge do corresponding groups need?

789. Different application of an existing process?

790. Who will fund the training?

791. Has the relevant business unit been notified of installation and support requirements?

792. How will the stakeholders share information and

transfer knowledge?

793. How can you best frame the message so that it addresses the audiences interests?

794. Where will the funds come from?

795. Will the culture embrace or reject this change?

796. What work practices will be affected?

797. What prerequisite knowledge or training is required?

798. Who might present the most resistance?

799. How do you know the requirements you documented are the right ones?

800. What is the most cynical response it can receive?

801. Clearly articulate the overall business benefits of the Digital Forensics project -why are you doing this now?

3.0 Executing Process Group: Digital Forensics

802. Will a new application be developed using existing hardware, software, and networks?

803. What type of information goes in the quality assurance plan?

804. Are the necessary foundations in place to ensure the sustainability of the results of the programme?

805. What are some crucial elements of a good Digital Forensics project plan?

806. How is Digital Forensics project performance information created and distributed?

807. What is the critical path for this Digital Forensics project and how long is it?

808. What are the main types of goods and services being outsourced?

809. What were things that you need to improve?

810. Contingency planning. if a risk event occurs, what will you do?

811. Who will be the main sponsor?

812. What is in place for ensuring adequate change control on Digital Forensics projects that involve

outside contracts?

813. How well did the chosen processes fit the needs of the Digital Forensics project?

814. How can software assist in Digital Forensics project communications?

815. What are the typical Digital Forensics project management skills?

816. Will outside resources be needed to help?

817. Does software appear easy to learn?

818. How do you enter durations, link tasks, and view critical path information?

3.1 Team Member Status Report: Digital Forensics

819. How will resource planning be done?

820. The problem with Reward & Recognition Programs is that the truly deserving people all too often get left out. How can you make it practical?

821. How can you make it practical?

822. What specific interest groups do you have in place?

823. How much risk is involved?

824. Are the attitudes of staff regarding Digital Forensics project work improving?

825. Are the products of your organizations Digital Forensics projects meeting customers objectives?

826. Does every department have to have a Digital Forensics project Manager on staff?

827. When a teams productivity and success depend on collaboration and the efficient flow of information, what generally fails them?

828. Will the staff do training or is that done by a third party?

829. Are your organizations Digital Forensics projects

more successful over time?

830. What is to be done?

831. Does the product, good, or service already exist within your organization?

832. Why is it to be done?

833. How does this product, good, or service meet the needs of the Digital Forensics project and your organization as a whole?

834. Do you have an Enterprise Digital Forensics project Management Office (EPMO)?

835. How it is to be done?

836. Does your organization have the means (staff, money, contract, etc.) to produce or to acquire the product, good, or service?

837. Is there evidence that staff is taking a more professional approach toward management of your organizations Digital Forensics projects?

3.2 Change Request: Digital Forensics

838. Can static requirements change attributes like the size of the change be used to predict reliability in execution?

839. Is it feasible to use requirements attributes as predictors of reliability?

840. Has a formal technical review been conducted to assess technical correctness?

841. What is a Change Request Form?

842. Who is included in the change control team?

843. How do team members communicate with each other?

844. Have scm procedures for noting the change, recording it, and reporting it been followed?

845. How are changes graded and who is responsible for the rating?

846. Change request coordination ?

847. How is the change documented (format, content, storage)?

848. Screen shots or attachments included in a Change Request?

849. How many lines of code must be changed to

implement the change?

850. Describe how modifications, enhancements, defects and/or deficiencies shall be notified (e.g. Problem Reports, Change Requests etc) and managed. Detail warranty and/or maintenance periods?

851. Will there be a change request form in use?

852. When do you create a change request?

853. What is the purpose of change control?

854. Are change requests logged and managed?

855. How to get changes (code) out in a timely manner?

856. Why were your requested changes rejected or not made?

857. What needs to be communicated?

3.3 Change Log: Digital Forensics

858. Is the change backward compatible without limitations?

859. When was the request submitted?

860. Does the suggested change request seem to represent a necessary enhancement to the product?

861. Should a more thorough impact analysis be conducted?

862. How does this change affect scope?

863. Is the change request open, closed or pending?

864. Is the requested change request a result of changes in other Digital Forensics project(s)?

865. Is the submitted change a new change or a modification of a previously approved change?

866. Is this a mandatory replacement?

867. Who initiated the change request?

868. Does the suggested change request represent a desired enhancement to the products functionality?

869. Do the described changes impact on the integrity or security of the system?

870. Will the Digital Forensics project fail if the change

request is not executed?

871. Where do changes come from?

872. How does this relate to the standards developed for specific business processes?

873. When was the request approved?

874. Is the change request within Digital Forensics project scope?

875. How does this change affect the timeline of the schedule?

3.4 Decision Log: Digital Forensics

876. Adversarial environment. is your opponent open to a non-traditional workflow, or will it likely challenge anything you do?

877. How consolidated and comprehensive a story can you tell by capturing currently available incident data in a central location and through a log of key decisions during an incident?

878. It becomes critical to track and periodically revisit both operational effectiveness; Are you noticing all that you need to, and are you interpreting what you see effectively?

879. Behaviors; what are guidelines that the team has identified that will assist them with getting the most out of team meetings?

880. How does the use a Decision Support System influence the strategies/tactics or costs?

881. How does provision of information, both in terms of content and presentation, influence acceptance of alternative strategies?

882. Is your opponent open to a non-traditional workflow, or will it likely challenge anything you do?

883. What alternatives/risks were considered?

884. Decision-making process; how will the team make decisions?

885. Does anything need to be adjusted?

886. How do you define success?

887. Who will be given a copy of this document and where will it be kept?

888. At what point in time does loss become unacceptable?

889. Who is the decisionmaker?

890. With whom was the decision shared or considered?

891. What is the line where eDiscovery ends and document review begins?

892. What is the average size of your matters in an applicable measurement?

893. What is your overall strategy for quality control / quality assurance procedures?

894. Meeting purpose; why does this team meet?

895. Is everything working as expected?

3.5 Quality Audit: Digital Forensics

896. Do prior clients have a positive opinion of your organization?

897. Is your organizational structure established and each positions responsibility defined?

898. Has a written procedure been established to identify devices during all stages of receipt, reconditioning, distribution and installation so that mix-ups are prevented?

899. How does your organization know that its system for recruiting the best staff possible are appropriately effective and constructive?

900. Is your organizational structure a help or a hindrance to deployment?

901. How does your organization know that its relationships with industry and employers are appropriately effective and constructive?

902. How does your organization know that its system for attending to the health and wellbeing of its staff is appropriately effective and constructive?

903. What does an analysis of your organizations staff profile suggest in terms of its planning, and how is this being addressed?

904. How does the organization know that its industry and community engagement planning and

management systems are appropriately effective and constructive in enabling relationships with key stakeholder groups?

905. How does your organization know that its range of activities are being reviewed as rigorously and constructively as they could be?

906. How does your organization know that its information technology system is serving its needs as effectively and constructively as is appropriate?

907. Are the policies and processes, as set out in the Quality Audit Manual, properly applied?

908. What has changed/improved as a result of the review processes?

909. How does your organization know that the range and quality of its accommodation, catering and transportation services are appropriately effective and constructive?

910. Is progress against the intentions measurable?

911. What happens if your organization fails its Quality Audit?

912. How does your organization know that its systems for providing high quality consultancy services to external parties are appropriately effective and constructive?

913. How does your organization know that its relationships with relevant professional bodies are appropriately effective and constructive?

914. Is there a risk that information provided by management may not always be reliable?

915. Have the risks associated with the intentions been identified, analyzed and appropriate responses developed?

3.6 Team Directory: Digital Forensics

916. Why is the work necessary?

917. Who are your stakeholders (customers, sponsors, end users, team members)?

918. Process decisions: are all start-up, turn over and close out requirements of the contract satisfied?

919. Do purchase specifications and configurations match requirements?

920. Process decisions: do invoice amounts match accepted work in place?

921. Who are the Team Members?

922. Have you decided when to celebrate the Digital Forensics projects completion date?

923. Who should receive information (all stakeholders)?

924. Process decisions: which organizational elements and which individuals will be assigned management functions?

925. Timing: when do the effects of communication take place?

926. Days from the time the issue is identified?

927. Does a Digital Forensics project team directory

list all resources assigned to the Digital Forensics project?

928. Who will report Digital Forensics project status to all stakeholders?

929. What are you going to deliver or accomplish?

930. Process decisions: how well was task order work performed?

931. Who will be the stakeholders on your next Digital Forensics project?

932. Who will write the meeting minutes and distribute?

933. Process decisions: are there any statutory or regulatory issues relevant to the timely execution of work?

3.7 Team Operating Agreement: Digital Forensics

934. Do you begin with a question to engage everyone?

935. What are the current caseload numbers in the unit?

936. Resource allocation: how will individual team members account for time and expenses, and how will this be allocated in the team budget?

937. Must your team members rely on the expertise of other members to complete tasks?

938. How does teaming fit in with overall organizational goals and meet organizational needs?

939. What are the boundaries (organizational or geographic) within which you operate?

940. How will you divide work equitably?

941. Does your team need access to all documents and information at all times?

942. Are there the right people on your team?

943. Conflict resolution: how will disputes and other conflicts be mediated or resolved?

944. Seconds for members to respond?

945. What is culture?

946. Have you established procedures that team members can follow to work effectively together, such as a team operating agreement?

947. Did you prepare participants for the next meeting?

948. Do you call or email participants to ensure understanding, follow-through and commitment to the meeting outcomes?

949. Confidentiality: how will confidential information be handled?

950. Methodologies: how will key team processes be implemented, such as training, research, work deliverable production, review and approval processes, knowledge management, and meeting procedures?

951. Do you upload presentation materials in advance and test the technology?

952. How will you resolve conflict efficiently and respectfully?

953. Are there influences outside the team that may affect performance, and if so, have you identified and addressed them?

3.8 Team Performance Assessment: Digital Forensics

954. To what degree are staff involved as partners in the improvement process?

955. When does the medium matter?

956. To what degree are sub-teams possible or necessary?

957. Do you give group members authority to make at least some important decisions?

958. To what degree do members articulate the goals beyond the team membership?

959. What do you think is the most constructive thing that could be done now to resolve considerations and disputes about method variance?

960. What structural changes have you made or are you preparing to make?

961. If you have criticized someones work for method variance in your role as reviewer, what was the circumstance?

962. To what degree is there a sense that only the team can succeed?

963. Individual task proficiency and team process behavior: what is important for team functioning?

964. To what degree can team members meet frequently enough to accomplish the teams ends?

965. If you have received criticism from reviewers that your work suffered from method variance, what was the circumstance?

966. To what degree do team members understand one anothers roles and skills?

967. To what degree does the teams work approach provide opportunity for members to engage in fact-based problem solving?

968. To what degree is the team cognizant of small wins to be celebrated along the way?

969. To what degree does the teams purpose constitute a broader, deeper aspiration than just accomplishing short-term goals?

970. To what degree are the teams goals and objectives clear, simple, and measurable?

971. Effects of crew composition on crew performance: Does the whole equal the sum of its parts?

972. To what degree can team members vigorously define the teams purpose in considerations with others who are not part of the functioning team?

973. To what degree do team members feel that the purpose of the team is important, if not exciting?

3.9 Team Member Performance Assessment: Digital Forensics

974. What were the challenges that resulted for training and assessment?

975. To what degree are the skill areas critical to team performance present?

976. What qualities does a successful Team leader possess?

977. What are acceptable governance changes?

978. What are the staffs preferences for training on technology-based platforms?

979. How often are assessments to be conducted?

980. Is there reluctance to join a team?

981. In what areas would you like to concentrate your knowledge and resources?

982. What is the target group for instruction (e.g., individual and collective or small team instruction)?

983. New skills/knowledge gained this year?

984. To what degree will new and supplemental skills be introduced as the need is recognized?

985. What makes them effective?

986. Are the goals SMART ?

987. What are the basic principles and objectives of performance measurement and assessment?

988. To what degree can all members engage in open and interactive considerations?

989. What are top priorities?

990. What is collaboration?

991. What stakeholders must be involved in the development and oversight of the performance plan?

3.10 Issue Log: Digital Forensics

992. Is there an important stakeholder who is actively opposed and will not receive messages?

993. What are the stakeholders interrelationships?

994. Is the issue log kept in a safe place?

995. What help do you and your team need from the stakeholders?

996. Do you have members of your team responsible for certain stakeholders?

997. Who were proponents/opponents?

998. Do you often overlook a key stakeholder or stakeholder group?

999. Are you constantly rushing from meeting to meeting?

1000. Which stakeholders can influence others?

1001. What is the impact on the Business Case?

1002. Who are the members of the governing body?

1003. Are they needed?

1004. What is a change?

1005. What effort will a change need?

1006. How is this initiative related to other portfolios, programs, or Digital Forensics projects?

1007. Do you feel a register helps?

4.0 Monitoring and Controlling Process Group: Digital Forensics

1008. Propriety: who needs to be involved in the evaluation to be ethical?

1009. What kinds of things in particular are you looking for data on?

1010. Does the solution fit in with organizations technical architectural requirements?

1011. Change, where should you look for problems?

1012. What were things that you did very well and want to do the same again on the next Digital Forensics project?

1013. What resources are necessary?

1014. How can you monitor progress?

1015. Who are the Digital Forensics project stakeholders?

1016. What input will you be required to provide the Digital Forensics project team?

1017. Feasibility: how much money, time, and effort can you put into this?

1018. What is the timeline?

1019. How well defined and documented were the Digital Forensics project management processes you chose to use?

1020. How was the program set-up initiated?

1021. How well did the chosen processes fit the needs of the Digital Forensics project?

1022. Is the program making progress in helping to achieve the set results?

1023. Are the services being delivered?

1024. How many potential communications channels exist on the Digital Forensics project?

1025. Is there adequate validation on required fields?

4.1 Project Performance Report: Digital Forensics

1026. How will procurement be coordinated with other Digital Forensics project aspects, such as scheduling and performance reporting?

1027. To what degree does the task meet individual needs?

1028. To what degree will team members, individually and collectively, commit time to help themselves and others learn and develop skills?

1029. What is the degree to which rules govern information exchange between individuals within your organization?

1030. What is in it for you?

1031. To what degree does the formal organization make use of individual resources and meet individual needs?

1032. To what degree are the goals ambitious?

1033. To what degree can the team ensure that all members are individually and jointly accountable for the teams purpose, goals, approach, and work-products?

1034. To what degree are the members clear on what they are individually responsible for and what they are jointly responsible for?

1035. To what degree are fresh input and perspectives systematically caught and added (for example, through information and analysis, new members, and senior sponsors)?

1036. What is the degree to which rules govern information exchange between groups?

1037. To what degree do team members frequently explore the teams purpose and its implications?

1038. To what degree can the cognitive capacity of individuals accommodate the flow of information?

1039. To what degree is the information network consistent with the structure of the formal organization?

1040. To what degree does the teams purpose contain themes that are particularly meaningful and memorable?

1041. To what degree does the information network communicate information relevant to the task?

4.2 Variance Analysis: Digital Forensics

1042. Are indirect costs charged to the appropriate indirect pools and incurring organization?

1043. When, during the last four quarters, did a primary business event occur causing a fluctuation?

1044. Do the rates and prices remain constant throughout the year?

1045. Budgeted cost for work performed?

1046. What is the budgeted cost for work scheduled?

1047. Is all contract work included in the CWBS?

1048. Why do variances exist?

1049. The anticipated business volume?

1050. Are there externalities from having some customers, even if they are unprofitable in the short run?

1051. Are there changes in the overhead pool and/or organization structures?

1052. Are all cwbs elements specified for external reporting?

1053. Are the requirements for all items of overhead

established by rational, traceable processes?

1054. How does the use of a single conversion element (rather than the traditional labor and overhead elements) affect standard costing?

1055. What does a favorable labor efficiency variance mean?

1056. Are there quarterly budgets with quarterly performance comparisons?

1057. Favorable or unfavorable variance?

1058. Are there changes in the direct base to which overhead costs are allocated?

1059. Is budgeted cost for work performed calculated in a manner consistent with the way work is planned?

4.3 Earned Value Status: Digital Forensics

1060. How much is it going to cost by the finish?

1061. When is it going to finish?

1062. Are you hitting your Digital Forensics projects targets?

1063. How does this compare with other Digital Forensics projects?

1064. Verification is a process of ensuring that the developed system satisfies the stakeholders agreements and specifications; Are you building the product right? What do you haverify?

1065. What is the unit of forecast value?

1066. If earned value management (EVM) is so good in determining the true status of a Digital Forensics project and Digital Forensics project its completion, why is it that hardly any one uses it in information systems related Digital Forensics projects?

1067. Earned value can be used in almost any Digital Forensics project situation and in almost any Digital Forensics project environment. it may be used on large Digital Forensics projects, medium sized Digital Forensics projects, tiny Digital Forensics projects (in cut-down form), complex and simple Digital Forensics projects and in any market sector. some people, of course, know all about earned value, they have used it for years - but perhaps not as effectively as they could have?

1068. Where are your problem areas?

1069. Where is evidence-based earned value in your organization reported?

1070. Validation is a process of ensuring that the developed system will actually achieve the stakeholders desired outcomes; Are you building the right product? What do you validate?

4.4 Risk Audit: Digital Forensics

1071. Is the customer technically sophisticated in the product area?

1072. To what extent should analytical procedures be utilized in the risk-assessment process?

1073. Do you have a procedure for dealing with complaints?

1074. What impact does experience with one client have on decisions made for other clients during the risk-assessment process?

1075. Estimated size of product in number of programs, files, transactions?

1076. Who audits the auditor?

1077. Do you conduct risk assessments on all programs, activities and events?

1078. Does the adoption of a business risk audit approach change internal control documentation and testing practices?

1079. Are requirements fully understood by the team and customers?

1080. Is your organization willing to commit significant time to the requirements gathering process?

1081. What is the anticipated volatility of the requirements?

1082. Does your organization communicate regularly and effectively with its members?

1083. Are Digital Forensics project requirements stable?

1084. Are auditors able to effectively apply more soft evidence found in the risk-assessment process with the results of more tangible audit evidence found through more substantive testing?

1085. Have all possible risks/hazards been identified (including injury to staff, damage to equipment, impact on others in the community)?

1086. How do you compare to other jurisdictions when managing the risk of ....?

1087. Does the implementation method matter?

1088. Are formal technical reviews part of this process?

1089. Are procedures developed to respond to foreseeable emergencies and communicated to all involved?

1090. Are contracts reviewed before renewal?

4.5 Contractor Status Report: Digital Forensics

1091. What was the actual budget or estimated cost for your organizations services?

1092. What was the overall budget or estimated cost?

1093. If applicable; describe your standard schedule for new software version releases. Are new software version releases included in the standard maintenance plan?

1094. How long have you been using the services?

1095. What are the minimum and optimal bandwidth requirements for the proposed soluiton?

1096. What is the average response time for answering a support call?

1097. Describe how often regular updates are made to the proposed solution. Are corresponding regular updates included in the standard maintenance plan?

1098. How is risk transferred?

1099. Are there contractual transfer concerns?

1100. How does the proposed individual meet each requirement?

1101. What process manages the contracts?

1102. What was the budget or estimated cost for your organizations services?

1103. What was the final actual cost?

1104. Who can list a Digital Forensics project as organization experience, your organization or a previous employee of your organization?

4.6 Formal Acceptance: Digital Forensics

1105. Who supplies data?

1106. How does your team plan to obtain formal acceptance on your Digital Forensics project?

1107. Was the sponsor/customer satisfied?

1108. Did the Digital Forensics project manager and team act in a professional and ethical manner?

1109. What is the Acceptance Management Process?

1110. Was the client satisfied with the Digital Forensics project results?

1111. What are the requirements against which to test, Who will execute?

1112. Do you perform formal acceptance or burn-in tests?

1113. Does it do what client said it would?

1114. Did the Digital Forensics project achieve its MOV?

1115. Do you buy pre-configured systems or build your own configuration?

1116. What was done right?

1117. Was the Digital Forensics project goal achieved?

1118. Was business value realized?

1119. Was the Digital Forensics project work done on time, within budget, and according to specification?

1120. What function(s) does it fill or meet?

1121. Have all comments been addressed?

1122. What features, practices, and processes proved to be strengths or weaknesses?

1123. Does it do what Digital Forensics project team said it would?

1124. Is formal acceptance of the Digital Forensics project product documented and distributed?

5.0 Closing Process Group: Digital Forensics

1125. What is the Digital Forensics project Management Process?

1126. Based on your Digital Forensics project communication management plan, what worked well?

1127. Were sponsors and decision makers available when needed outside regularly scheduled meetings?

1128. What is an Encumbrance?

1129. What areas were overlooked on this Digital Forensics project?

1130. Was the schedule met?

1131. Did the Digital Forensics project team have enough people to execute the Digital Forensics project plan?

1132. Does the close educate others to improve performance?

1133. What is the amount of funding and what Digital Forensics project phases are funded?

1134. How critical is the Digital Forensics project success to the success of your organization?

1135. Did the Digital Forensics project management methodology work?

1136. Specific - is the objective clear in terms of what, how, when, and where the situation will be changed?

1137. Can the lesson learned be replicated?

1138. What were the desired outcomes?

1139. What will you do?

1140. How well did the chosen processes fit the needs of the Digital Forensics project?

1141. How dependent is the Digital Forensics project on other Digital Forensics projects or work efforts?

1142. What were things that you did well, and could improve, and how?

5.1 Procurement Audit: Digital Forensics

1143. Do your organizations policies promote and/or safeguard fair competition?

1144. Was the pre-qualification screening for issue of tender documents done properly and in a fair manner?

1145. Months to reflect any changes in policy?

1146. Were no tenders presented after the time limit accepted?

1147. Are blank purchase order forms protected?

1148. Does your organization use existing contracts where possible to avoid the cost of bidding?

1149. Are advance payments to employees properly authorized and controlled?

1150. Does your organization maintain a current file of vendors and vendor catalogues?

1151. Are sub-criteria clearly indicated?

1152. Are there regular reviews and analysis of the performance of the procurement function/unit?

1153. Is there a forum where the departments suppliers performance is regularly considered with the suppliers?

1154. Is a physical inventory taken periodically to verify fixed asset records?

1155. Could the bidders assess the economic risks the successful bidder would be responsible for, thus limiting the inclusion of extra charges for risk?

1156. Does the strategy ensure that appropriate controls are in place to ensure propriety and regularity in delivery?

1157. Are buyers prohibited from accepting gifts from vendors?

1158. Are approval limits definitive as to amount and classification of expenditure?

1159. Can small orders such as magazine subscriptions and non-product items such as membership in organizations be processed by the ordering department?

1160. Does the individual approving disbursements sign or initial the document?

1161. Is there a policy on purchasing from users of organization products?

1162. How is the evaluation of contract performance organized?

5.2 Contract Close-Out: Digital Forensics

1163. How/when used ?

1164. Has each contract been audited to verify acceptance and delivery?

1165. Have all contracts been closed?

1166. Why Outsource?

1167. Was the contract sufficiently clear so as not to result in numerous disputes and misunderstandings?

1168. How does it work?

1169. What happens to the recipient of services?

1170. Change in circumstances?

1171. Are the signers the authorized officials?

1172. Have all acceptance criteria been met prior to final payment to contractors?

1173. Change in knowledge?

1174. Parties: who is involved?

1175. Parties: Authorized?

1176. Have all contracts been completed?

1177. Have all contract records been included in the Digital Forensics project archives?

1178. Change in attitude or behavior?

1179. Was the contract type appropriate?

1180. How is the contracting office notified of the automatic contract close-out?

1181. Was the contract complete without requiring numerous changes and revisions?

1182. What is capture management?

5.3 Project or Phase Close-Out: Digital Forensics

1183. Which changes might a stakeholder be required to make as a result of the Digital Forensics project?

1184. Planned completion date?

1185. Who controlled key decisions that were made?

1186. What are the marketing communication needs for each stakeholder?

1187. Were the outcomes different from the already stated planned?

1188. What information is each stakeholder group interested in?

1189. When and how were information needs best met?

1190. How often did each stakeholder need an update?

1191. Is the lesson significant, valid, and applicable?

1192. Was the user/client satisfied with the end product?

1193. Were cost budgets met?

1194. Who controlled the resources for the Digital

Forensics project?

1195. Did the Digital Forensics project management methodology work?

1196. Were messages directly related to the release strategy or phases of the Digital Forensics project?

1197. What information did each stakeholder need to contribute to the Digital Forensics projects success?

1198. What was learned?

1199. What is a Risk?

1200. What are the mandatory communication needs for each stakeholder?

1201. How much influence did the stakeholder have over others?

1202. What process was planned for managing issues/ risks?

5.4 Lessons Learned: Digital Forensics

1203. What things surprised you on the Digital Forensics project that were not in the plan?

1204. Is there a clear cause and effect between the activity and the lesson learned?

1205. How accurately and timely was the Risk Management Log updated or reviewed?

1206. What was helpful to know when planning the deployment?

1207. If issue escalation was required, how effectively were issues resolved?

1208. What skills did you need that were missing on this Digital Forensics project?

1209. How objective was the collection of data?

1210. How was the political and social history changed over the life of the Digital Forensics project?

1211. How much of your time was spent on other than this Digital Forensics project?

1212. How clearly defined were the objectives for this Digital Forensics project?

1213. Who needs to learn lessons?

1214. Did the delivered product meet the specified

requirements and goals of the Digital Forensics project?

1215. Was there enough support – guidance, clerical support, training?

1216. Did the Digital Forensics project change significantly?

1217. How adequately involved did you feel in Digital Forensics project decisions?

1218. How efficient were Digital Forensics project team meetings conducted?

1219. Why does your organization need a lessons learned (LL) capability?

1220. Whom to share Lessons Learned Information with?

1221. Was any formal risk assessment carried out at the start of the Digital Forensics project, and was this followed up during the Digital Forensics project?

Index

258

283

9 780655 516163